Owning a Racehorse

Diane Harvey

Foreword by John Biggs

J. A. Allen

London

British Library Cataloguing in Publication Data
Harvey, Diane
  Owning a racehorse.
  1. Racehorses. Care & management — manuals
  I. Title
  636.1'2
  ISBN 0-85131-466-X

Published in Great Britain by
J. A. Allen & Company Limited,
1, Lower Grosvenor Place, Buckingham Palace Road,
London SW1W 0EL

For my parents who gallantly tried, but sadly failed, to put me off horses, and for Apple who ensured my continued fascination with, and special love for, the Thoroughbred.

Contents

		Page
	LIST OF ILLUSTRATIONS	viii
	FOREWORD	x
	ACKNOWLEDGEMENTS	xi
	INTRODUCTION	1
1	Types of ownership	3
2	Which trainer?	13
3	Which horse?	23
4	Naming your horse	49
5	Choosing your colours	51
6	Vaccination	54
7	Jockeys and jockeys' riding fees	57
8	Types of race	60
9	A day at the races	74
10	If things go wrong	79
11	When the horse is finished on the racecourse	83
12	Books the racehorse owner will find helpful	93
13	Questions on racing	98
14	Useful addresses	115

List of Illustrations

	Page
The Thoroughbred racehorse is not really pet material	2
A leg each	5
While you are arguing	9
Your horse will live very well	15
Are the staff cheerful?	16
He may not have the experience	20
If the trainer feels the horse has no potential	21
Points of the horse	22
All sorts of defects could be lurking	26
Black type categories	29
Leave the ear lobe pulling and nose scratching	32
Pedigree of Prince Khalid Abdullah's Dancing Brave	39
A parrot mouth	42
Conformation of the forelegs	44
Conformation of the hind legs	44
Straightness of leg	45
Some examples of racing silks	52
The virus still remains one of the mysteries	56
Steeplechasing is a sport for the brave	63
Nursery races	64
Free to enjoy yourself	74
Ask an assistant to find the jockey	76
Do not give any riding instructions to the jockey	76
If you cannot afford to be patient	79
Its dressage test phase leaves something to be desired	85
If the mare has cow hocks	89
Suddenly they turn up with some money	105

List of Plates

1   Pre-sale inspection at Tattersalls

2   A yearling filly

3   A yearling filly

4   A yearling colt

5   A Tattersalls auctioneer

6   Two of trainer David Thom's horses

7   Trainer James Bennett supervises the schooling of one of his steeplechasers

8   Owners and trainers in the paddock

Foreword

People buy racehorses for a variety of reasons but, in the main, they hope that their particular horse will be successful and that it will give them some fun.

Miss Diane Harvey, herself a racehorse owner, points out the problems and pitfalls which may present themselves particularly in the early stages of racehorse ownership. The potential owner will find this Guide invaluable. The advice is given with humour and it is clear – problems notwithstanding – that Miss Harvey is still an enthusiast.

JOHN BIGGS
Director General of the Racehorse Owners' Association

Acknowledgements

My warmest thanks go to John Biggs, Director General of the Racehorse Owners' Association, for the foreword and for his valued advice; to Peter Spruce for the photographs and encouragement; to Chris Moore, Guy Dearman, Neville Hicks and Nikki for their good-natured tolerance, and special thanks to my expert contributors; Charles Nelson, Sue Cameron and Terry Jennings.

Introduction

The decision to become the owner of a Thoroughbred racehorse should not be taken lightly. It will impose a substantial financial burden upon the purchaser, who, once the horse has been bought, will then also receive regular sizeable bills for the horse's upkeep and training. It is a pastime that can cost more than you may care to spend. However, the cost is an aspect of racehorse ownership that most people are well aware of, and presumably, if you could not afford it, you would not be considering it. That said, there are less expensive ways of getting involved in owning racehorses.

At this stage, before any money has changed hands, it might be prudent to examine your reasons and motives for buying a racehorse.

Are you intent on seeking fame and glory and getting your name in the history books of the Turf achieved through the excellent physical endeavours of an animal? If this is the case, then remember that it is highly unlikely that you will buy a Turf superstar on your very first attempt. The vast majority of racehorses fill the bottom tier of racing with comparatively few making the heady heights of Group One calibre. At these lower levels there is real fun to be had, but little glory.

Or perhaps you are an animal lover who happens to have a few thousand guineas to spare on an unusual pet. Unfortunately, the Thoroughbred racehorse is not really pet material and racing is an industry, where the Thoroughbred is the essential cog in the wheel. But if you are looking for excitement, beauty, speed and power in a hobby, then owning a racehorse may fit the bill exactly.

This book is not so much a guide for the top bracket income people or for those lucky few with their white-railed stud paddocks filled with potential Classic winners, because such

1

. . . the Thoroughbred racehorse is not really pet material . . .

people can obtain the best professional assistance, although I hope they will find particular sections of this book helpful. I am aiming this book more towards the enthusiast with a lower income who is hankering after a chance to point to a horse cantering down to the start of a humble maiden race, and be able to say 'That's mine, or at least bits of it are!'

The next few pages attempt to explain what you will be facing if you pursue your intended course of action. Purely on grounds of economy of words I have referred to owners, breeders, lads, trainers and jockeys etc., as 'he' when of course an increasing number of 'shes' are involved in all aspects of racing, so the term 'he' is not intended to be sexually discriminating.

At the time of going to press, the Jockey Club Rules were as stated, but readers should note that the Rules are updated and revised every year towards the end of March and should amend details accordingly.

1 Types of Ownership

Individual Ownership

Several roads can lead you into racehorse ownership. If you are hoping to share the cost of owning a horse, then make sure that you are in with people that you can get on with and trust, and who preferably have more experience than you in this area. Be wary of answering advertisements for shares offered in the racing press, as the people will be strangers and you will have missed out on the exciting and crucial stage of choosing your own horse. Such advertisements are mostly totally straight-forward and honest, but the odd one may be a disguise for an owner trying to get rid of a no-hoper. Do not part with any money until you have done your research and, if in doubt, do not be persuaded to part with a penny against your better judgement. Sharing the costs is obviously enticing and may be the only way that you can afford to be involved, but be careful, there is no need to rush into anything. People who sell horses can be more persistent and sharper than the proverbial used car salesman for trying to sell their wares, but do not be railroaded into something that you might regret, probably sooner rather than later.

The oldest and still the most popular type of ownership is by the individual, the rich individual. It is prohibitively expensive to buy a potentially decent animal and to put it in the care of one of the top trainers, and if the fact that the vast majority of horses are owned by this sort of owner tends to make you think that racehorse ownership is the rich man's prerogative, you would be right.

If you have calculated a few prices and worked out a few sums and decided that you will only be able to afford a horse if it can subsidise itself with prize money, then you cannot afford to own

3

a racehorse. Only a very small percentage of the horses in training actually win, and fewer still actually win enough to pay for themselves or make any decent contribution. If you cannot enter into ownership ready to pay all bills unaided, then sharing ownership may be the answer for you.

To help you to pay all the bills that will start to amass as soon as you decide to go into ownership, Weatherbys, the administrators for the Jockey Club, offer owners an accounting service for payment of such things as fines, registration fees, entry fees and declaration fees etc. The above is termed a 'forfeit account' because failure to settle bills will lead to the owner's name being added to the forfeit list. The accounting services may be extended to include payment of trainer's and jockey's fees. Prize money is automatically paid into this account. Pratt and Co. (accountants for the Turf) offer a similar service to that provided by Weatherbys.

As an extremely rough guide, you can expect to part with a sum in the region of £9,000 on the annual maintenance and keep of your horse, not including the initial purchase price (which can range from around 1,000 guineas to several million), entries, travel costs etc. There is also 15 per cent V.A.T. on training fees.

There are a few ways, less costly than outright individual ownership, of obtaining a form of racehorse ownership now permitted by the Jockey Club, these being: partnerships, syndicates, companies, clubs and leasing.

Partnerships

Partnerships can consist of up to four people and the partners' names are published in the *Racing Calendar*. Also they will all be registered as owners under Rule 40 of the Rules of Racing with Weatherbys in Portman Square, London W1, and in Wellingborough, Northants. The considerable paperwork involved in registering is designed to ensure that disqualified or 'warned off' persons do not get back into ownership, having been disqualified for behaviour that the Jockey Club regards as unacceptable under the Rules of Racing. Behaviour such as racing a horse under rules and in 'flapping' or unrecognized amateur races at the same time, or more simply because the Jockey Club considers the applicant 'unsuitable'.

If you all have an equal share (a leg each!) then you should also have an equal say in planning the horse's campaign, but partners will automatically have a say in their horse's future regardless of the size of their share. It might be wise to set out an agreement that you all sign to put minds at rest on such matters as: will you all be guided by the trainer's advice? Does the horse still run if not all of the partnership can attend the meeting? Do you only run the horse at courses close to the owners' home areas? Do you automatically offer your share to your partners if you want to withdraw etc?

It is not always wise to have the trainer as a partner. The fact that he wants to be a partner reflects the trainer's opinion of the horse, but it also makes it awkward if the rest of you lose faith in

. . . a leg each . . .

him and want to move the horse to another trainer. It can also lead to unrest amongst his other owners, who may suspect him of giving preferential treatment to the horse. If the trainer keeps a share himself he may be tempted to sell it if approached, thus allowing a stranger into the group of owners. This may or may not please the other owners, although they too are, of course, just as entitled to sell their shares.

Remember that all partners are equally liable for any charges that might arise as transgressions of the Rules of Racing, the latter being revised and updated each year. The liability under the Rules of Racing is also legally binding in common law if liability can be established. A company is permitted to make up one of the four places in a partnership, generally appointing an agent to represent them.

If a member of the partnership is depressed by the horse's performances then the partnership may be re-formed, redistributing that share, or be dissolved with the horse being put up for auction. Auctioning the horse is the final solution to ending a partnership that is winding down, perhaps due to the horse's repeated failure in the lowest company. If you attend the sale to see your horse sold, then be warned that, for some unknown reason, your horse will never have looked so good as when you see him in the sale ring masquerading as a racehorse. But do not be tempted to buy him in again unless you think the others have misjudged the horse hopelessly. Try to remember why you agreed to sell him, and do not look at the wounded expression on his face! Also bear in mind that it is unwise to be the under-bidder on your own horse just to push the price up. It would be suitably embarrassing for you if you placed the final bid and had to buy the horse back in for more than you originally paid for him, especially if you really wanted to be shot of the creature.

Tattersalls in particular do not permit bidding by a single vendor, issuing a written prohibition which reads as follows: 'No vendor shall in any circumstances whatever bid or allow any agent or other person to bid on his behalf for any lot owned by such vendor, whether individually, in syndicate or in partnership, save that this restriction shall not extend to lots stated in catalogue to be Partnership Property.'

However, under-bidding seems to be a pretty regular

occurrence at the sales, with people prepared to take the risks to ensure a better price for their wares.

The Extended Partnership (previously called a Syndicate)

If you owned a quarter share in a partnership, then the extended partnership, which came into effect at the start of the 1989 Flat season, offers you a smaller share, up to a twelfth share. This is obviously a cheaper way to spread the costs, but the effect is often nullified by the syndicate owning several horses, sometimes mixing Flat and National Hunt horses so that the owners have their interest and their money held throughout the year.

To begin with you will probably be asked for a lump sum of one-twelfth the animal's value, plus monthly training fees on top. If you are asked for 600 guineas up front, check in the sales' reports for the price for which the horse was bought. If the price paid was markedly less than 7,200 guineas, then it is obviously not going to be a very good deal for the members. The total price for the members is bound to be slightly more than the sale price to cover some expenses, but excessive pricing up is a bad sign and is unlikely to be followed by value for money. As long as you are told the dam's name, the horse can be traced through the sales.

Expenses can be reduced by having a horse in Ireland owing to the fact that V.A.T. is not added on to the purchase or sale of horseflesh, nor on to training fees. The only disadvantage for non-Irish residents being extra expenses to see the horse at the yard and on the racecourse. If owners like to see their horses often, then the lack of V.A.T. will be insufficient incentive to those facing journeys across the Irish Sea on a regular basis.

All twelve partners will be required to register as owners with Weatherbys, and to have entered into a Training Agreement with their trainer. The smaller owner is, therefore, treated as a true owner whereas the old syndicate only required four of its members to be registered as lessees. The new partnerships require each member to open an account with Weatherbys. Again, as with the ordinary smaller partnership, a private formal agreement should be drawn up amongst syndicate members to avoid squabbles later, particularly over the reallocation of shares.

The Jockey Club produces a Partnership Name form which

7

will be used on entries and racecards. Once completed, this form should be sent to Weatherby's registration department. Each member should possess a copy of the completed document. Your horse cannot run until this has all been satisfactorily completed. Professional help with the old form of syndication was essential because it came under the jurisdiction of the Financial Services Act, and errors were very expensive. The extended partnership should ease this problem.

Obviously, as the number of owners increases for individual animals, so the sense of involvement decreases. It is worth remembering that in the desirable event of your horse passing the post in front of his opponents, you may not be allowed into the winners' enclosure if numbers are limited, and there will be twelve of you battling ungraciously over four owners' badges, and sometimes only two badges at courses like Lingfield, Doncaster and Stratford. Some more helpful courses will however give more than four badges if asked in advance. The next battle will concern who should lead the animal into the winners' enclosure for the glorious applause (unless yours was an unfancied outsider beating the hot favourite, in which case there may be no applause, merely a hostile hush).

While you are arguing, the horse will probably side-step the affray and make his own way in, glancing disapprovingly in your direction from time to time. So try to get turns organised in advance.

When your eye has been blacked and your nose bloodied from several similar scenes, then you may decide to sell your share and opt for the quieter life. The registration department must be advised of your sale within 48 hours. If the fight for the lead rope got really out of hand, and one of your shareholders died, then the registration department should be told the sorry news within 28 days! Any changes in membership or circumstances should also be reported as soon as possible. The Jockey Club Stewards may withdraw their approval of a particular partnership member at any time, cancelling the registration of the syndicate, and eliminating the horse from racing, so it does pay to make sure that your members are all 'desirable' types, otherwise your ownership can be terminated before it has really begun. This underlines the fact that you should know your members before you set it up.

. . . while you are arguing . . .

The Company

With ownership by a company, an authorised individual must be registered at Weatherbys in addition to the company itself. The company shareholders actually own the horse. The registration department may want to look at the company's register of members, the names of the Directors and of the Company Secretary, the annual balance sheet, profit and loss accounts etc. before recognising the company's application. Companies owning racehorses may be affected by the new Financial Services Act which may require legal advice as even the Jockey Club seems uncertain of its relevance.

The Inland Revenue regards ownership of racehorses as a hobby activity. Therefore, it stands outside the tax net; winnings will not be taxable as income, but, by the same token, racing costs are not allowable. Companies tend to embark on racehorse ownership as a means of advertising and promoting their goods and services. If both the Inland Revenue and H.M. Customs and Excise are satisfied with the *bona fides* of the company, the capital cost of the horse and the training costs and other related expenses may be set off as legitimate costs of the

9

business; V.A.T. on training fees etc would be recoverable. Should a company find itself in disagreement with the Inland Revenue or Customs and Excise, it is possible to lodge an appeal with the local Commissioners (for revenue issues) or with the V.A.T. Tribunal (for V.A.T. matters).

Club Ownership

A fifth type of ownership is club ownership. These 'clubs' are seen regularly advertised in the racing press offering shares in horses already acquired and probably with a trainer. However, to be able to offer shares in horses, these clubs must in fact be companies which just call themselves clubs. The real clubs will not initially offer shares in horses as this would not be allowed under Jockey Club rules. To begin with, one would join a club for the visits and competitions that they offer. At a later date – several years after the club's formation – the club may indeed offer shares in racehorses which it will then be entitled to own. A club should not be set up for the express purpose of owning race-horses. There seems to be no limit to the number of shareholders some of these clubs will take, which means that you could own a tail hair! Military units and ships' companies etc. may be regarded as clubs by the Jockey Club if such groups wished to enter into racehorse ownership.

Clubs can only offer long distance ownership. You may be more involved than the average racegoer, but you are one of a crowd and your trainer may never know your name. In this multi-ownership you may have little or no say in where the horse will run, and, as the owners will be dotted around the country, it will be an impossible task to choose a course close to all owners' home bases. Sadly, your horse will not know you from Adam.

Club ownership is available at the discretion of the Stewards of the Jockey Club for clubs which have been in existence for two years and whose main activity is unconnected with racing. Thus, a local cricket club may decide to buy a horse and it is quite likely that the Jockey Club would accept its registration as a 'club' owner. The Rules of Racing do not recognise racing clubs which are usually an adjunct of Thoroughbred and breeding companies. The companies have shareholders and the 'club' offers additional benefits such as a tipping service and visits to racecourses and training yards.

For the genuine club owners, i.e. clubs acknowledged by the Jockey Club, the rules for the club must be submitted to the Jockey Club with the Trust Deed, and up to four Trustees should be proposed. The horse will run under the name and colours chosen by the club.

These clubs must pose a dilemma for the trainer. He wants the extra horses in his yard, but not the extra people who descend on the stables to visit en masse, churning up the lawn and blocking the exits. However, the clubs are usually quite good at arranging trips and visits which are of interest to the racing fan, e.g. visits to other stables, the National Stud, the National Horseracing Museum etc.

If you are afraid of crowds and do not like queueing to see your horse, then do not give up. The clubs can vary tremendously in size, and with a little time and effort, you should be able to find something that suits your pocket and your preferences for small groups. Word of mouth, via personal recommendation is still the best way to get into a suitable group.

Leasing

The last form of ownership is not really ownership; it is the lease, and leasing is a means of acquiring the use of a horse for little or no capital outlay. A lease may be granted to an individual, a partnership, a company or a club, any one of which would then have to register in the normal way. As the lessee, you pay all costs to put the animal in training without actually buying it, although there may be a leasing fee. Written agreement should be obtained between lessee and lessor with regard to prize money distribution (be optimistic) length of lease, option to buy etc. The lessor is usually the breeder of the horse in question.

Do be wary of owner/breeders who tell you that they have for lease next year's champion grazing in their fields amongst the cows, barbed wire and discarded hiking boots. Ask yourself why, if a horse is so good, does the owner want to lease it out anyway? It would be worth your while to research the horse's background; who were his sire and dam? It goes without saying that if only one or neither parents appear in the General Stud Book, and it cannot be proved that they are Thoroughbreds, then the offspring cannot race under Rules on the Flat, but may race over jumps in some cases.

If the prospective racehorse is being used to pull a cart and to compete in the local gymkhana with the farmer's daughter then you might be wise to lease someone else's horse, but then, there have been a few rags to riches stories in racing . . . more than a few.

Having decided what form your ownership will take, it is time to look for a trainer.

2 Which Trainer?

Choosing a trainer is only mildly less risky than choosing a horse. I am assuming that you will be looking for a public trainer, i.e. one who trains the horses of several owners instead of having one, all-powerful owner, as in the case of some of the Arabs and the rich aristocracy of years gone by.

There are three types of training licence; a licence to train hurdlers and steeplechasers only; a licence to train horses to race on the Flat only and a dual purpose licence which covers both. Additionally, a permit trainer may train hurdlers and steeple-chasers, but only for himself or for his immediate family. Not all owners like to bet and the same applies to trainers. If you are not a punter, you are unlikely to be satisfied in a betting yard so find out before you decide.

You can begin to sift through the available trainers at the racecourses. Look to see how trainers turn out their runners and lads in the paddock. Stables that regularly win the prize for the best turned-out are obviously taking a lot of time, trouble with, and pride in, their horses. Look for neatness, tidy plaits in the mane, level quarter marks etc., putting yourself in the position of the judge for best turned-out. However, the proof of the pudding is in the eating, and the prettiest turn-out is rather meaningless if the trainer has no winners. Horses that look workmanlike and can do their job are preferable to the useless beauties. Each time a trainer runs a horse, it acts as an advertisement for his stable, and therefore the smartness and efficiency of both man and horse will attract new customers.

Publications such as the *Trainers' Record* and the *Sporting Life Trainers' Review*, will help you to assess the success rate of particular trainers. Trainers with a lot of winners from a few horses are particularly noteworthy and warrant close inspection. *The Directory of the Turf* will tell you to whom the trainer was assistant, i.e. from whom he learnt.

You may also be attracted by the trainer's choice in horses. Some trainers like a definite stamp of horse, and you can often name the trainer of an animal in the paddock, without referring to the racecard, simply by the sort of horse it is.

A trainer will influence his lads with his kind of horsemanship. Lads who handle their horses with quiet firmness are a good advertisement for the stable, but lads who yank on the poor creature's mouth as they lead it around the paddock are not going to attract any new owners to the stable.

Flat trainers who worry about a fall in the number of Group One winners in their yards are likely to be the most expensive with whom to keep a horse. They often have a waiting list of owners trying to place their horses with them. Your two-year-old could be a bit long in the tooth before you get him into one of these stables, and you will have to take out a second mortgage on the house to pay the training fees. If, however, the trainer accepts your horse, he must think it worth a chance, which is in itself flattering because such men can afford to be choosey.

Although your horse will live very well in such a place, remember that the most successful trainers take in huge numbers of horses spread around several yards, and you may find that it is the assistant trainer who is actually working on your horse. Good as he may be, you might feel a little put out that your horse is not receiving the attention of the person who you are paying to do the job. It is rather like going to one of the top hairdressing salons and having a trainee practise on you. However, delegation is the reward for success, and whoever is in charge of your horse will still be answerable to the trainer. Realistically, the trainer with 150 horses or more in his care will be physically unable to supervise them all, and the main concern is the results of the training system employed by each individual trainer.

The problem with deciding on a trainer is increased by the fact that they do not advertise their rates. You will not be able to select a short list of trainers by looking at the training fees they charge unless you call up each one and ask, and then they may not divulge their prices over the telephone. As a general rule trainers in Newmarket and Lambourn tend to have the higher price tags, due mainly to the higher costs, the tradition and better facilities of these areas. Trainers further north are at a

14

. . . your horse will live very well . . .

disadvantage when it comes to attracting the wealthy owners. This is owing to geographical reasons rather than any lack of ability because most of these owners are based in the south. Northern trainers' prices will be that much cheaper, but would probably work out equal once you have added on the extra petrol used to visit the yard if you are not from the north yourself.

When you have selected a few trainers, go and see them. Arrive a little earlier than arranged and have a good look around the yard while you are waiting. You are looking for signs of an efficient, happy yard. Are the staff cheerful? Do the horses **look fit and well cared for? Are the stable buildings safe and well ventilated with lots of light? Is the bedding on the stable floors clean and dry whether it is straw, peat, shavings or newspaper?** Have a check list of questions prepared for the trainer with regard to fees and extras so that you gain a clear idea of what it would cost you to join him.

Surprisingly, a lot can be gleaned about a yard from its muck

Are the staff cheerful?

heap, although I do not advocate too close an examination! A well run yard will have a tidy, concrete-walled area for depositing manure, and have the heap removed regularly when the area is full. If most of the manure is trailing around the yard, then it shows a lack of effort on the part of the staff which might manifest itself in other areas of their work with more disastrous effect. Some stables have 'pebble lawns' which the lads are expected to rake into place daily; it looks lovely, but is a little excessive when it comes to tidiness and is a waste of manpower. Above all, the stable should be an effective working unit. Do not be put off by stables that house a horse and a goat together. This does not indicate a lack of stabling space, but is an old trick for providing a rather nervous and highly-strung Thoroughbred with comforting companionship. One should spare a thought for the poor goat who has to share a confined space with a psychotic horse.

It will also help you to pick the right trainer if you are honest with yourself about what sort of owner you are likely to be. For example, will you want to see the horse every other day and drive a busy trainer to distraction by your interference? Is the cost most important to you? Are you a betting person first and a horse owner second? Is a local trainer essential or are you prepared to travel? Do you want to share a trainer with a friend, etc?

Betting trainers are those who subsidise their cheaper training fees with betting coups, hopefully with the owners in on the fun. The problem is finding out if the trainer is a betting man. Some will regard the enquiry as an insult, others as the highest praise! Trainers may be a little reserved when it comes to sharing stable tips, especially with a new owner who may not have the sort of horse that would contribute to the stable income in this way. You have to be as sharp as they are to avoid missing out on a 'good thing'.

In general, it pays to get to know the lad who 'does' your horse, i.e., the one who feeds, grooms, mucks out and generally tends to the animal's needs. He may also exercise the horse. Find out his name, when his birthday is and what his favourite alcoholic beverage is for Christmas. The lad is the one person who really gets to know your horse, literally inside out and end to end. He may profess to love the horse like his own child; this may be true but generally the bigger the present, the greater the love! Befriend the lad and you will be rewarded with real inside information, (or ridicule, depending on the lad's opinion of owners). Some of the best lads will welcome your honest interest in the horse which is probably regarded as more theirs than yours. You only pay the bills.

On the subject of bills, you will be staggered by the sort of things for which you will find yourself writing cheques, including; training fees, tack, farrier, veterinary bills, entry fees, declaration fees, travelling costs, gifts to the staff (compulsory), clipping, gallop maintenance, dentist, jockey retainer and fee, insurance etc.

It is essential at the start of your association with your trainer that you sign a 'Training Agreement' on a specially designed form and this must be registered on payment of a fee by the trainer. This training agreement sets out the cost of the basic training fee and advocates definition of the extra charges made above the basic cost.

Should the trainer increase his training fee, the owner must be advised by recorded delivery and given three weeks to accept or reject the rise in costs. If the owner sees the increase as excessive, then the existing agreement will stand, or the horse may be moved elsewhere. Whilst this issue is being debated, the horse cannot run.

Trainers are entitled to report their owners to the Stewards of the Jockey Club if training fees are not paid within three months of having been presented. If the owner's defence is unacceptable, he will find himself on the forfeit list thirty days after the Stewards' decision, and he would then be 'warned off' the turf i.e. denied the right to own or run a racehorse under rules.

A few trainers regard owners as a necessary evil and you may not find a welcome in the hillside when you visit. In this case, latch on to his assistant trainer or his secretary to ensure that you are not totally ignored, or, better still, choose another trainer. A good trainer should be a businessman and a diplomat; his business is to train horses and to keep owners happy or risk losing them.

By placing his horse with a small yard, the first-time owner will receive very personal attention and a solid introduction to the sport. A good trainer will guide his owner through the intricacies and paperwork to ensure that he gets what he pays for; the thrill of possessing a Thoroughbred racehorse without all the worry.

It will add to your enjoyment if you can see your horse at different times in his working day; in his stable, working on the gallops, schooling, swimming etc. Your trainer should be happy to co-operate as long as you are able to fit in with his time-table.

Your trainer will ask you to sign an 'Authority to Act' to enable him to make entries on your behalf. It also gives him the power to decide on the action to be taken if the horse sustains a broken leg or other injury. This is a boon for the inexperienced owner, but if an owner does know something about racing, then, although the 'Authority to Act' has been signed, he may wish to work *with* the trainer when making the entries. It costs money each time a horse is entered, and if the animal is unlikely to be ready for a race, then a knowledgeable owner may be able to save himself some money.

A Newmarket trainer was reputed to have entered one owner's horse in 23 races in one week. One hopes the horse finally competed in the right race as the trainer was obviously taking a good deal of trouble choosing the races!

If you do not sign an 'Authority to Act' you must make the entries yourself.

Entries used to be made 21 days in advance with declarations at four days and at the overnight stage. The new five day entry system helps to reduce costs because the trainer will be able to enter a horse more accurately, knowing that the horse will be fit to run in five days' time. He will also find it easier to forecast the state of the going.

When making arrangements with your trainer to see your horse work, it is essential that you keep to the agreed time, to avoid upsetting the work timetable of an entire string. If the trainer has booked the gallops for a particular time, he will, understandably, not be pleased if you hold everything up. Your horse's training will suffer, and there is a greater risk of injury if fresh Thoroughbred racehorses have to stand around waiting and getting over-excited.

Seeing your horse work can be a mystifying affair if the trainer has not talked you through the aims of the gallop and what he will be looking for. You will invariably not see a dress rehearsal for the forthcoming race because the horse will probably be worked over a shorter distance than the target race, and with a different weight. This is because racehorses, like athletes, train at a lower level than that which they will ultimately be expected to attain.

The horses working with your newcomer will probably be older, experienced horses and may, therefore, be handicapped by a little extra weight in order to give your horse a chance to prove himself. These horses act as pacemakers; if your horse can run well against them, this will prove his ability and whether or not he is ready to enter a race.

It will also help you to know if your horse's rider is an experienced work rider, because a lad new to the game may have little say in the speed at which the horse is travelling for two reasons: 1) he may not have the experience and skill to assert the right amount of control over the horse, or, 2) the trainer may have to dictate the speed at which the horse is to be run, because, again, the rider may not yet have the experience to pace the horse himself.

. . . he may not have the experience . . .

Any potential a horse displays at home on the gallops may not be reproduced on the racecourse; many horses are happy to run at home, but do not settle down easily at the course. If a young horse does not impress on his first piece of work, it may indicate that the animal is indeed useless, or may just need more time. There is still hope for a youngster who showed early speed in his work gallop. A potential champion should be given all the time in the world, the mediocre animal should be raced early on if possible, before all the big guns are brought out. The early two-year-old prize money is very low and hopefully will not attract the top class competition. This is when your mediocre horse will have a chance of winning. Deciding just how early to run will be governed by the horse's physical and mental development.

If the trainer feels the horse has no potential he should be honest enough to tell you when this lack of ability has been proven, and to tell you when it is time to get rid of the horse, to avoid wasting any more money. This should be done before the horse's inability to run is made apparent on the racecourse, thereby making the horse difficult to sell when it comes on the market.

If the trainer feels the horse has no potential . . .

The owner who has become attached to the horse will find this a difficult time, especially if he is prepared to give the horse another try and the trainer is adamant about replacing it. The hardest pill to swallow would be to see the horse flourish and improve out of all recognition under someone else's ownership.

An owner should heed the trainer's advice to sell because it is professional opinion, and is not intended as a personal insult to the owner. It is a difficult decision for the trainer to make because if the owner agrees to sell and gives up racing totally, he loses a customer. The trainer gambles that the owner will sell and get another horse. Should the owner decide to do this then the trainer will be the ideal man to help choose the next horse, as he will try to choose something that he will be happy to train and the owner happy to own.

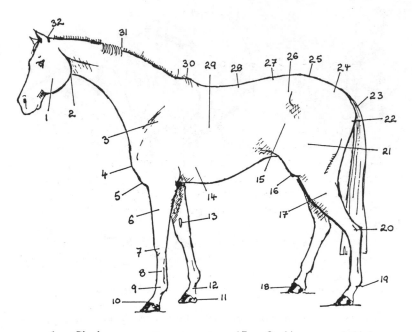

1.	Cheek	17.	Gaskin – second thigh
2.	Jowl	18.	Wall of hoof
3.	Shoulder	19.	Ergot
4.	Point of shoulder	20.	Hock
5.	Breast	21.	Thigh
6.	Forearm	22.	Point of buttock
7.	Knee	23.	Dock
8.	Cannon bone	24.	Croup
9.	Fetlock	25.	Point of croup
10.	Coronet	26.	Point of hip
11.	Heel	27.	Loins
12.	Pastern	28.	Back
13.	Chestnut	29.	Chest
14.	Chest – ribcage	30.	Withers
15.	Flank	31.	Crest
16.	Stifle	32.	Poll

Points of the horse

3 Which Horse?

The selection of your horse will be the most crucial choice that
you make as an owner, especially if funds limit you to pinning all
your hopes on just one horse. If this is the case, then you must
acquire the best that you can within these financial limits by
employing the assistance of a good trainer or bloodstock agent.
The next door neighbour who keeps a few ponies will not suffice
in this instance as expensive mistakes can be made when buying
Thoroughbreds for racing.

Having hunted down a good trainer or agent, remember that
he may be a good judge of a particular type of horse (potential
early-maturing two-year-olds, for example) but if this is not
what you have in mind, it would be advisable to find another
trainer who specialises in the type of horse you want.

You will have a choice of age of horse, from foals up to grand
old brood mares, depending on which sale you attend or which
breeder or private vendor you go to. Age must also be taken into
consideration when deciding what the horse will be destined for.

If you regard yourself as a horse person and know slightly
more than just which end bites and which end kicks, then you
might enjoy the challenge of choosing your own horse from one
of the big bloodstock sales at Newmarket's Tattersalls,
Ballsbridge Tattersalls (Ireland), or perhaps the Doncaster or
Ascot sales. Alternatively you could buy from abroad, but the
animal's stay will be limited by the rules of purchase. These state
that an owner importing a horse into Great Britain from abroad
will be required to pay V.A.T. on the purchase price unless the
horse is to be exported again within two years of the initial
purchase. However, H.M. Customs and Excise has recently
been authorised to extend this limit by six months in some cases
for temporarily imported yearlings.

Over the years you have presumably acquired a taste for

23

either the Flat or National Hunt racing, and your choice of horse will be governed by this. There is a light-hearted rivalry between the advocates of the different types of racing, rather like the Army's opinion of the Navy and vice versa. You become categorized as either a National Hunt 'sportsman' or a Flat race 'businessman'. It is apparently overlooked by these factions that they are all enthusiastic followers of racing as a sport, relishing the athletic beauty of the racehorse whatever their preference.

If your first love is freezing your digits off on a gale-battered National Hunt course, with the raindrops trickling onto your nose from the brim of your hat, or with the horses just discernible through sleet or snow, then you can choose between a ready-made animal i.e., a horse with race experience, in which case his rate of success will determine his price, or, if you are patient, you can have the added pleasure and expense of being involved early on and watching a young horse mature and prosper before your very eyes. The ultimate is the 'grow your own' approach, where you witness the animal first drop to the ground of your foaling box much to the surprised relief of your broodmare.

Breeding racehorses is not the sort of hobby for the faint-hearted, the squeamish or the non-wealthy.

It is worth remembering that the National Hunt horse can be turned away in the summer months and is therefore cheaper to keep during this period of the year. However, the longer season and higher risk of injury and subsequent veterinary bills may bring the cost up to the same level of expenditure as for the Flat racehorse.

Flat racehorses are working when the grass is good, and rest when the fields are bare and waterlogged, so they will require extra feeding and attention all year round and are never cheap to keep. The most economical way is for the horse to take his holiday in a paddock on his owner's property when his season is over, but if this is not feasible, then there are yards which specialise in livery for the recuperating racehorse, but at a price. Alternatively your trainer may let the horse stay on at the training stables, but you may still receive most of the same bills as when the horse was actually in training, apart from such things as travel and entries etc. It would be worth your while to have the horse yourself, if you have the facilities and are knowledgeable about stable management or have competent

24

staff, because you then get to know the animal itself as opposed to just being an infrequent visitor and bill payer. Knowing the animal's idiosyncracies adds to the owner's pleasure in and understanding of the horse. It also makes the trainer's life that bit easier because the owner will be made very aware of his horse's less desirable habits, and will not be surprised by the horse's antics when it goes back into training.

Buying a horse for the Flat can be approached in a similar way to purchasing his National Hunt colleague; by obtaining a made horse (unlikely to be cheap if at all decent) or by getting a youngster, maybe as young as a foal. However the latter is a challenge for the well tutored eye and should not be attempted by amateurs unless they have the funds to cover their mistakes.

So how do you track down the next Dancing Brave? You will be trying to acquire a horse through one of the following means: via a public auction, via a bloodstock agent, from a selling or a claiming race, or from a private vendor. Alternatively, your trainer may have a few horses in his yard that he bought, intending to find owners for them later. The disadvantage of choosing one of these already acquired animals is that your choice is severely restricted in comparison with attending an auction. However, if you do not have much idea as to what you would be looking for at an auction anyway, then it might be suitable for you to buy one of the trainer's horses. He presumably had enough faith in the horse to buy it in the first place with his own money. Ask to see the horse worked seriously on the gallops if he has reached that stage in his training. A lot of horses can look impressive when just cantering, but a good study of the gait you are interested in most is essential. Do not be satisfied with a look at it standing in the stable with its rugs and bandages on. All sorts of defects could be lurking under such concealment.

Another alternative is to buy direct from the breeder or vendor of an older horse, having perhaps seen the animal advertised for sale. Again, take your expert with you. No matter how much he charges for his expertise, it can save a lot more money in the end.

If the lure of the sales is too strong for you, and it can be an exciting experience, then I would recommend that you attend one of the reputable bloodstock auctions previously mentioned.

All sorts of defects could be lurking . . .

The sales actually take place between September and December for the yearlings, but sales of horses in and out of training are also held during the year. Attend several, before you take your cheque book with you, to get the feel of the atmosphere so that you avoid getting caught up in the auctioneer's hypnotic enthusiasm and launch into a buying frenzy. It helps if you keep an eye on the price bidding boards where bids are converted from guineas into various other currencies. The amounts in sterling usually have a sobering effect.

Before you go there to buy, it is best to establish your credit with the sales company as a new customer. They will need time to check with your bank, so the request should be made to allow time for this, unless you buy through an agent or trainer who will hold credit with the sales company.

If you are looking for a potential hurdler or steeplechaser, then it might be wise to go to a 'Horses in Training' sale, where horses that probably have some race experience will be available. Buying an untried yearling would require patience, money and great judgement if it is to grow into anything resembling a steeplechaser or hurdler in the future. A National Hunt horse will require courage, strength and stamina, all of which are difficult qualities to assess in a sale ring, so it can be helpful to follow a few horses already in training, watching them run and then approaching the owner or trainer with an offer, or waiting for the horse to appear in a selling or claiming race, if he is running at that low level, so that you can buy him at the racecourse; that way you know what you are buying. Some trainers will buy horses and race them ownerless in their own name, using the animal to advertise itself. This method of buying cuts down on some of the risk and the expense in the long run, because you will have bought a horse that has proved that it can do its job.

If you decide to go to a sale, your trainer may not feel able to make a good choice for you, so he may use the services of a bloodstock agent. Reputable agents will be members of the Federation of Bloodstock Agents (G.B.) Ltd., based in Gloucestershire. Such agents will require 5 per cent of the sale price; if an agent asks for a larger percentage, it would tend to indicate that he is not a member of the Federation. Bloodstock agents are paid to be the best judges of Thoroughbred horseflesh and should be the most experienced buyers of horses in existence. Some may specialise within their field, e.g. an agent may have an excellent eye for buying yearlings that will make up into decent two-year-olds.

However, some long-established agencies prefer to deal with established people in the racing industry, and require a personal introduction for new clients, so, as a newcomer, you may have trouble securing the services of an agent, unless your trainer introduces you. The more modern agencies ignore this dated approach and welcome new custom direct.

Agents not only buy horses, but can also act as your manager for your racing affairs and will liaise with your trainer if you cannot bring yourself to do so. A bloodstock sales company may be able to help you select a good agent if you are unable to make an intelligent choice yourself, as they obviously know all the agents from experience.

So let us assume that you are ready and eager to begin the search for the horse of your dreams. If you follow the pattern of most Flat racehorse owners, then you will be looking for a yearling at the sales. The first step is to buy the sales catalogue which lists all the horses that will be offered for sale. The second step is then to read the Conditions of Sale at the front or back of the catalogue, depending on the sales company format. (Sales abroad may have conditions that differ from those in Great Britain.) Your trainer or agent will then peruse the catalogue with you, marking off the likely candidates that have the sort of pedigree you are after (which will be given to the third generation), and that might be in the sort of price range you had in mind, remembering that V.A.T. will sometimes be added to the purchase price. The price is almost impossible to estimate until you actually see the horse in front of you. A rough guide is the fee, which is called the nomination fee, that the breeder paid to send his mare to the stallion. Stallion fees can be found in *The Stallion Book* and *Sires for* . . . (the relevant year) or direct from the stud standing the stallion. The breeder can worry with good reason if his stock only makes the nomination fee, or less.

If you are buying a Flat racehorse purely for the pleasure that it will give you, then you will probably be buying a sprinter. The international visitors to the sales are not too interested in sprinters as a rule because sprinters are bred a great deal abroad, so the bidding should be less competitive. Hopefully the horse will be racing for you soon and probably quite regularly through the season, health permitting. Thus a sprinter is probably the ideal buy for the fun-orientated owner.

Stayers may be slightly less attractive propositions because the prize money for the average stayer is minimal. There is also a little more international interest in this type of animal at the top of the tree, so the prices will reflect this. The American buyers are not particularly interested in this category of horse as it would have very little racing opportunity in the States. If Americans *are* buying, it would suggest that they will be racing the horse in Europe or perhaps Japan.

Buying a stayer will mean a longer wait for the horse's debut on a racecourse because stayers need time to mature and are raced at an older age than sprinters, so the keen and impatient owner may find it a frustrating animal to own. It is also probable that a stayer will not race as often as a sprinter.

The more popular class of horse with the foreign buyers is the horse destined to run over seven to twelve furlongs as this is a suitable animal to place in Pattern races. All nationalities will be bidding and you may find yourself a little out of your depth.

The best pedigree does not ensure the best individual, and the horse's conformation will be the first thing that provokes you to have a closer look, or to walk away, shaking your head knowledgeably!

The Auction

In the Tattersalls' sales catalogue, 'black type' indicates winners of particular types of race. There are four styles of type that can appear in the catalogue. The horse's name given in the boldest black type with upper-case letters indicates the winner of a European Pattern race, Listed race, a foreign Graded Stakes race or a major American Stakes race. If the horse's name is in slightly lighter black type using upper- and lower-case letters, then it signifies that the horse was placed in one of the above types of race. Names depicted in italic capitals show that the animal has won a Flat race, and ordinary upper- and lower-case letters indicate that the horse is a winner of a National Hunt race, or has not won at all. Other bloodstock sales companies employ slight variations in their allocation of black type, so be sure to read the catalogue carefully.

Black type races

Horses included in this catalogue are printed in one of the four styles below.

HAMMER —winner of a European Pattern Race, a Foreign Graded Stakes Race, a Listed Race or a Major American Stakes Race.

Hammer —a placed horse in the above races. N.B. Fourth places included for Pattern Races and Foreign Graded Stakes Races only.

HAMMER —a winner of a flat-race.

Hammer —a winner of a N.H. Race or a non-winner.

Black type categories

29

The advantages of attending a public auction are that you have a much greater choice, and there is the opportunity for comparison all in one place. The auction ring will be protected from the elements, and buyers can sit in relative comfort, wickedly fluttering their eyelashes at the auctioneer and his assistants from time to time to add to the confusion of the bidding.

Once you have marked off some likely animals, you will have to wait patiently for the day of the sale to arrive. On sale day it is advisable to get there early and to start looking at the lot numbers that you have marked in your catalogue. This is where you can reduce your list of possibles to a more manageable number, as you note with disappointment the pathetic individual that made such good reading in the catalogue.

Professional producers of horses for the sales will know all the tricks of the trade to present their produce to the best advantage. *Caveat emptor* means 'the buyer beware', and is a very relevant maxim for the purchase of horses. Horses with definite physical faults will be presented in such a way that their failings will be concealed where possible, whilst the best qualities in the animal will be extravagantly highlighted. If a horse has a short neck, it can be made to look longer by putting lots of small plaits in the mane, although yearlings and foals are not plaited. Poor quarters can be camouflaged to some extent by quarter marks and patterning, and incorrect legs can be disguised by standing the horse out unsquare. If a horse has a tendency to swing a leg out instead of moving straight (dishing), then the shrewd handler will set a steadier pace when the horse is trotted out to minimise this faulty action. Your veterinary surgeon will be able to tell you if there are any more serious problems to be found, but, again, the more ruthless vendor can dupe the professionals. For example, if a horse comes to the sales lame on his off (right) foreleg, it is not unknown for a disreputable vendor to mask this by laming the near (left) foreleg as well, thus making the horse lame on both forelegs and making it difficult to detect the lameness, as the horse will favour neither leg. However, most of the people selling their horses at the sales will be respectable horsemen trying to make a living.

Your friendly expert will come into his own now as he assesses the conformation and temperament of each horse. He will be looking for an animal whose shape and construction is such that it will survive the rigours of training and racing and is generally built for the career that it will pursue. Remember, a large percentage of horses never see a racecourse and are as useful to their owners as overgrown hamsters that sit in their cages all day, having to lie down periodically to get their breath back after a spin on the exercise wheel!

Now you have made your final selections from the catalogue and from seeing the lots, and are sitting comfortably by the ring-side impatient for the auction to begin. The auctioneer mounts his platform and introduces the first lot, which is led around the ring, the artificial lighting giving the horse's coat a stunning sheen. It is the auctioneer's unenviable task to arouse interest in each lot, trying to raise each horse's price up to at least beyond its reserve. He will not tell you what the reserve is, but he will let people know if there is no reserve. He will also declare if a horse is a crib-biter, windsucker or weaver, as these vices all lead to difficulties in putting on and keeping condition on a horse and will affect its training. It pays to visit the horses in their boxes before the sale to assess such habits, although the shock to the horse of being in a new stable in a new yard with lots of strange horses and people may temporarily make him forget about his stable vices.

It is easy to be mesmerised by the seemingly endless stream of horses in and out. but stand by your selection list, even if you see one in the ring that you think you must have missed originally. You probably did see it and ruled it out on some grounds. In any event, you will not have the opportunity to see the animal in detail before bidding if you leave it this late.

When your chosen horses start to come in, stick determinedly to the limit that you set yourself, ignoring the auctioneer's emotional blackmail, with cries of 'Don't lose him for a bid sir!' and 'You'll be sorry if he wins the Derby!' Do not be bullied and do not try to find out who you are bidding against as it may frighten you into giving up if it is a big name, or you may find that there is no other bidder and the auctioneer is trying to raise you above the reserve. As long as you are not tempted to exceed your limit, it really does not matter who your competitor is in the sales ring. If you are badly situated by the ring it can help to draw attention to your bid to catch a bid spotter's eye and keep

31

that eye contact until you give up bidding. Make your bids obvious, because too subtle an approach might not get you noticed. Raising a hand or your catalogue are the standard ways to get the auctioneer's attention. Leave the ear lobe pulling and nose scratching signals to the regulars.

Leave the ear lobe pulling and nose scratching . . .

Most of the auctioneers in this country produce an atmosphere of an equine equivalent to a Sothebys sale. Others are quite dynamic to watch and listen to and seem to cajole buyers to spend that bit more. These livelier auctioneers are attracting quite a fan club with the vendors who are getting better prices for their animals due to this more forceful form of selling. It is sometimes possible to outbid a rival, by making one bid over a round number. For example, agents often have instructions not to go over a round limit of, say, 5,000 guineas, so a bid of 5,100 guineas would win the horse.

If you are lucky and manage to get one of your short-listed horses for as near to the price as you intended, then write your name on the purchaser's slip and return it to the auctioneer's clerk.

From the moment the hammer falls, the horse becomes your responsibility, unless you want a re-examination by a veterinary surgeon. The horse does not come complete with luggage and transport, but the vendor will probably let you have him with his headcollar if he is feeling generous, which he often is not, so it is essential that you bring travelling equipment with you including rugs, bandages, poll and tail guards, hock and knee boots, all of which should be supplied by your trainer if you are working with one. You do not want your horse's career to end before it has even begun because of an avoidable injury in the horsebox. If you have not brought a horsebox or trailer with you, then there are usually boxes for hire. Alternatively, you can pay for the horse to be kept at the Sale's stables for a day or two while you make arrangements for his collection.

It is a good idea to get the horse insured immediately for his purchase price, which will be in guineas and include V.A.T., and then alter that once he has gained or lost value on the race-course. There are companies that specialise in bloodstock insurance who frequent the big sales. Some owners do not insure their horses at all. It is more expensive for obvious reasons to insure a jumper than a Flat racehorse. As with any form of insurance, it is worth shopping around to get the best quotes. Horses are usually insured for loss of use i.e. irreparable injury or death, because loss of use is much dearer and difficult to prove. If a racehorse injures himself to the extent that he will never be up to racing again, but can still be hacked-out, then the insurance company may not pay out, because the horse can still be used in some form, even if not for the original purpose for which it was purchased. It is therefore essential to know what your horse's insurance policy will pay out on. The company may require an autopsy before paying out on the death of a horse. It can be cheaper to insure a yearling than an older horse. Geldings are more expensive to insure, as they are rather unkindly regarded as being more expendable. Basically, if losing the horse would put a financial strain on the owner, then it is worth while to insure against such an eventuality. An owner that has fewer financial worries may choose not to insure.

Requests for re-examination by a vet must be made up to an hour after your bid was accepted. If during this examination the horse is found to be unsound, then the sale does not go through. Any subsequent complaints should be reported immediately or within 48 hours, followed by written confirmation to be on the auctioneer's desk up to 72 hours after the sale. Complaints of unsoundness should be presented with a veterinary certificate.

One week is the time limit for reporting faulty pedigrees, rigs (a male horse whose testicles have not descended normally), undeclared vices and operations e.g. tubing. All the rules for selling and buying horses at auction are set out in the catalogues and they must be read very carefully before you attend the sale.

Assessing a horse's temperament is difficult just by looking at him. The main clues are his eyes, ears, legs and teeth. If you see the last two heading your way at speed, then he is probably not a very nice animal to handle, but he may run like the wind, if only he will agree to co-operate. Looking into a large kind eye is reassuring for both man and beast, and a lot can be gleaned from the look in the eye. If the ears are constantly back, then the horse is either annoyed or in pain, or it can mean that he intends to inflict pain on someone else. Nervous horses will find it difficult to settle to their work and may not do themselves justice on the racecourse, and steady, placid animals may need a lot more hard work to inspire them to sparkle.

Buying from the Racecourse

If you decide to buy from the racecourse i.e. via a claiming or selling race, (in the latter case the winner of the race is immediately put up for auction in the winner's enclosure) then you will at least have had the chance to assess the animal's action and ability to do its job. Selling-platers (inferior racehorses) are unlikely to improve far beyond that class, and you may be buying a horse who will probably have a limited talent, although a clever trainer could get one or two wins out of him. There is, however, an unwritten rule amongst most trainers that they will not claim or bid for a horse entered in these races because they do not wish to take work away from a fellow trainer.

Some smaller trainers have only selling-platers in their yards and have to enter their horses in this type of race in order to stand a chance of winning, despite the fact that they know they will probably lose the horse if it wins.

A horse that wears blinkers or a visor is not necessarily a rogue as is often thought. The use of such equipment may be perfectly innocent in assisting a horse to concentrate on the business in hand instead of admiring the view.

The main point to consider when buying a horse is to buy one that you can live with. You have to own it, and it will eat just as much whether it is a good or a bad one. Neither the trainer nor the lad will thank you for sending them a lunatic, besides, if it is pretty and sensible, you could always retire it to the show ring if it shows no aptitude for racing.

Get your treasure safely installed in his new home and start dreaming while you wait to see what you have actually bought, just a horse, or a racehorse.

Pedigrees

Understanding and following pedigrees is a popular sport in itself, especially amongst Flat race enthusiasts, owing to the fashions in the bloodstock market for particular stallions. Stallions' offspring are statistically analysed each year, placing the stallion on a top sire list according to his success as a sire in the eyes of the industry. Do not be too swayed by such things, as genetic principles apply as much to horse breeding as to any other species. The Thoroughbred breeder is a gambler, taking his chances with the laws of genetics. He must attempt to forecast what will happen when he puts his mare to a particular stallion.

Statistics are wonderful things but are entirely open to varying interpretations. Predictions made through statistical methods can be confounded by the existence of various phenomena. For example, there is an observed tendency for statistical predictions to regress toward the mean, or average, of the characteristic measured. The sons of very tall fathers tend to be less tall, and the sons of very short fathers tend to outgrow their fathers. Or, in racehorse terms, very fast sires tend to produce less fast offspring and vice versa.

Sires do tend to produce horses that have similar distance preferences, but there are always exceptions. Kris, for example, won over distances ranging from five to eight furlongs, but has sired offspring that have won over fourteen furlong trips. Known Fact also won over distances from five to eight furlongs as a two- and three-year-old, and he too has sired offspring winning over the longer trip. Mansingh, a sprint specialist winning over five furlongs at two years old, has produced ten-furlong horses, but over 50 per cent of his winning progeny have been winning over five furlongs, so the exceptions prove the rule where the unexpected longer distance horses are fewer in number than the sprinters sired by this particular stallion. Of course the dam would also exert her influence on the offspring, so stayers produced by a cross with Mansingh, for example, may reflect a greater influence by the dam.

The pedigree will be of value when used in conjunction with the conformation and temperament. The pedigree is the horse's family tree. The last three generations will be displayed in sales catalogues as well as the racing and breeding successes of the first, second and third dam (i.e. mother, grandmother and great grandmother). You will be looking for parents and grandparents who pass on the desirable characteristics of speed, stamina, temperament and soundness. Sires and dams who have produced winners are sought after and therefore their offspring will be more expensive. Some people will pay more attention to the stallion, believing that he will have a stronger influence on his progeny than the mare. Others favour the mare. Of course the laws of genetics state that the foal will have half of his dam's genes and half of his sire's. The dominance or recessiveness of these genes will determine what characteristics the animal will display, for example, if the stallion is bay and the mare chestnut, and the gene for bay is dominant, then the offspring will be bay in three out of four instances when the same sire and dam are mated. It is assumed that the athletic ability is also passed on in this way (or the passing on of 'energy' as Federico Tesio, the master breeder and trainer put it), but athletic parents will not guarantee an athletic offspring, and racehorses should be athletes first and foremost.

In some cases it has, however, been found that certain strains or family lines of Thoroughbreds produce their best offspring when crossed with each other. This is known as a 'nick'. Breeders who believe they have discovered a nick will repeat such crosses anticipating a better than average chance of success.

If you are buying on a budget, then pedigrees can help focus the attention on the sort of animal that might make a precocious two-year-old, leading hopefully to a rapid return on your initial investment, because the horse can run early on and ideally win back some of its purchase price. Look at youngsters bred from sprinting lines, or from parents who were early maturing sorts themselves. You can find such things out by the brief racing career highlights in the sales catalogue, or by more in-depth research, consulting back issues of *Timeform* annuals, *Statistical Record* annuals and form books. To find the stallion's racing record you will have to use one of the latter methods because the catalogue only carries such information on the mares, presumably assuming that everyone knows all about the stallions. However, Tattersalls catalogues have a sire index in the front, and, in the Doncaster catalogues, the index is on the yearlings' page. Geldings obviously have no propagation potential, so their performances are more important than their pedigrees.

Do not get too bogged down with pedigrees. Just think of your own family. Do your siblings all share the same talents? Were you all sporty at school? Offspring of the same union are all very different due to the genetic lucky dip involved in the production of a zygote (embryo). Pedigree devotees will pay vast sums for horses that are closely related to proven racing successes. It is worth bearing in mind the old adage that lightning never strikes twice in the same place and close blood ties with success do not guarantee success.

When one hears the family of the horse being referred to, the term is applied to the female line. Horses by the same sire are not really regarded as related because of the large number of horses a stallion will sire, but horses out of the same dam are referred to as half sisters or half brothers. Full brothers and sisters are by the same sire out of the same dam.

The example pedigree is of the 1986 hero Dancing Brave, the horse that caught everyone's imagination. The sire (father) is shown above the dam (mother) on pedigrees. Dancing Brave would be described as being a bay colt by Lyphard out of Navajo Princess. All pedigrees are read from left to right; the top line is called the 'sire line' or 'tail-male line' and the lower line is the 'dam line' or 'bottom line'.

A 'good' pedigree is one which shows racing talent in close relatives. Some people are swayed by the appearance of a particular horse's name, like St. Simon, occurring several times in the pedigree. A geneticist would worry about this, regarding the horse as being too inbred to avoid weaknesses in make-up. Indeed close inbreeding with St. Simon has often resulted in horses that share his notorious bad nature.

All Thoroughbreds descend from the three foundation sires of the breed, the Darley Arabian, the Byerley Turk and the Godolphin Barb, who produced their own respective lines in Eclipse, Herod and Matchem, so no Thoroughbred can escape a history of very close inbreeding, however genetically unsound.

The best way to judge a pedigree must be to examine a horse's close relatives to assess their racing records and to then hope that the resulting offspring have inherited their most favourable qualities.

Equine geneticists working in America have estimated that the inheritance of racing ability influenced by genetics is between 30 per cent and 40 per cent and by environment 60 per cent to 70 per cent. If this is the case, then a lot more of the responsibility for racing success rests on the shoulders of the trainer who turns the equine raw material into racehorses.

On some racecards you may see horses marked with 'pedigree untraced'. It is an unlikely occurrence with Flat racehorses, but is sometimes seen with National Hunt horses. It means that one side of the pedigree cannot be traced back to its origins in the *General Stud Book*. A mare of note, with an untraced pedigree, is the game little hurdler turned steeplechaser Mrs. Muck. The only disadvantage of this is that if you plan to breed from this untraced line, you may find people a little wary of the unknown.

38

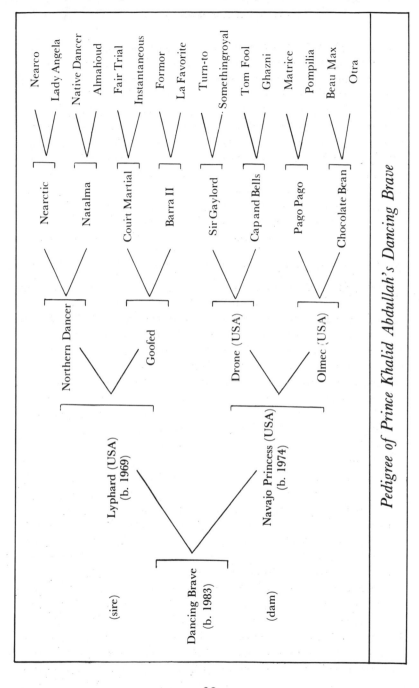

Pedigree of Prince Khalid Abdullah's Dancing Brave

As a rule, if you are buying a sprinter, he will probably be a compact individual with speed in his pedigree, either on one or both sides. A speedy stallion covering a stamina mare can still produce a sprinter. All you can do with pedigrees is 'guesstimate' how good the horse will be in comparison with his breeding. Science has enabled us to tell what sort of horse we have i.e. a stayer or a sprinter, by looking at the muscle fibre structure under a microscope, where rapid contracting muscle denotes a sprinter and slow contracting muscle denotes a stayer. However, most owners tend to assess this in the more conventional way from the pedigree and conformation, and then wait and see what happens on the gallops and the racecourse.

Conformation

Conformation, or the shape of the horse, is an extremely important factor that should not be overlooked, no matter how good the animal's pedigree appears in the sales catalogue. The ideal shape for a racehorse has yet to be seen, although several animals have been nominated over the years as coming close to perfection, including The Tetrarch, and Tesio's Nearco. Bearing in mind that perfection does not exist one must get as close to it as one can, especially with the legs and feet. In this endless search for perfection it is perhaps useful to remember that even the great Dancing Brave was rather a coarse, parrot-mouthed individual.

The structure of the horse is such that he is continually poised for flight, effectively standing on the equivalent of our middle finger. For an animal of his size, the weight bearing area is extremely small and the legs are thus potentially fragile and prone to strain. Leg and foot problems are the cause of most troubles, especially in the racing industry where the horse will spend a lot of time running much faster and more often than he was really designed for. In racing, we are utilising the horse's survival instinct, that is, if in doubt, run away as fast as you can.

When choosing a horse, one should select the animal whose structure lends itself to the discipline that it will be used for. Large thick bones are not suitable for a racehorse because such bone is heavy and is better suited to animals that pull carts rather than carry jockeys. Strong bone is essential, but it must be

40

quality bone, i.e. strong yet light. Horsemen tend to talk about a horse having 'bone', referring to the width of the cannon bone which is the bone that runs between the knee and fetlock joints. A racehorse will not require as much bone as, say, a heavy-weight hunter who will need more bone to carry his seventeen stone burden all day in the hunting field. A general purpose riding horse with good bone will measure approximately eight or nine inches around the cannon bone. The racehorse carries less weight and therefore needs less width of bone. The overall view of the horse must give the impression of fitting together nicely. If the back end does not seem to be suitable for the front end, e.g. too broad, too high etc, then the horse will lack balance, and the horse must have balance to be an efficient mover.

The following are a few guidelines to use when looking at the conformation of a racehorse.

The horse should have the look of a potential racehorse. If as a youngster he looks like a racehorse already, then there may be no room for improvement later on and he may actually regress. The Thoroughbred should be recognisable from other breeds of horse by its very fine coat, lean, long frame, refined head and long athletic limbs. The Thoroughbred has its neck set on lower than some breeds, giving greater mobility of the neck which contributes to the effectiveness of the gallop. Some Thorough-breds will display the slightly dished or concave face of the Arab horse that played such a large role in the creation of the Thoroughbred as a breed. Other Thoroughbreds will have straight and even convex profiles. All are acceptable.

Big young horses are usually clumsy horses until they have learned how to use themselves properly. Large two-year-olds tend to be all legs and no brain, and getting the two to co-operate can be a long and accident-ridden road! A handsome head is a bonus, but not essential, unless you intend to turn him into a show hack at the end of his racing career. The head should be so shaped that there is plenty of space for the nostrils to dilate widely for the maximum intake of oxygen. The shape of the jaw can affect the way that a horse is bitted. If he is uncomfortable with a bit in his mouth, then you may find it difficult to track down a jockey willing to ride him without steering and brakes. Hackamores or bitless bridles are of no use on a racehorse, as

41

they act on the horse's nasal passages, thus blocking out oxygen and perhaps losing the horse the race. The shape of the mouth not only affects the bitting of the horse, but also the horse's ability to eat effectively. A horse with a parrot-mouth (overshot jaw) cannot eat properly and, therefore, cannot utilise food to its best advantage.

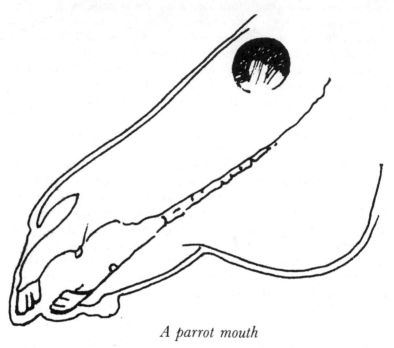

A parrot mouth

The way that the head is set onto the neck will also affect the way in which the horse will carry himself. If the head is set on in such a way that the horse has a very high head carriage, it will lead to an uncomfortable ride for the jockey who will not be able to assume his usual race-riding position, thus making him less effective.

You will be looking mainly for long lean lines to the horse's body which will facilitate the stretch of the legs during locomotion. Long hind limbs and well angled joints are required to maximise the propelling action of the hind legs.

Cold hard limbs are a mark of soundness and are much sought

after. Heat in the leg is a sure sign of a problem. A good walk can often give an insight into how well the horse will gallop as both these gaits are in a four-time beat, i.e. the legs come to the ground one at a time. A good walk is one where the horse swings his quarters rhythmically and tracks up behind, placing his hind feet in the hoofprints of the forefeet. A horse that potters along at the back will be a 'busy' horse to ride, using more energy going up and down rather than in surging forward. The way the legs emerge from the body will also dictate his action to some degree.

Young horses grow sporadically and lopsidedly, so that the withers may be higher than the croup, and then the croup higher than the withers at varying stages of development. A mature horse should be level at the croup and withers when fully grown, so do not reject a youngster for not being level on his top line; he should level out in time. A long back is weaker but more comfortable for the rider, a short back is less prone to strain, but can lead to a jolting ride. However, the raised position of the jockey will alleviate most discomfort for both man and horse.

A good length of rein, i.e. a good length of neck, is essential as the head and neck act as balancing agents for the horse's body when in action, and can mean the difference between first and second place in a tight finish. The way in which the head and neck are set onto the shoulder will indicate how the horse will carry himself. A sloping shoulder set at approximately 45 degrees from the vertical is desirable for effective locomotion. The stride should be economical and a workmanlike action is preferable to a flashy action that wastes time and energy in a race. A low or 'daisy cutting' action is usually more successful on firmer going, whereas a higher knee action tends to have the advantage in heavier going. Unfortunately, there is no opportunity to see a horse's action at an auction other than his walk and trot unless he breaks loose from his handler! Some of the bigger studs are now making videos of their young stock so that interested parties can view these in advance of the sale and see the animal at liberty in a paddock, kicking up his heels.

There should be a good depth of girth with plenty of room for the heart and lungs to expand when they are under stress in a race. The horse with an inadequate girth depth will appear very leggy and unsubstantial. The way the legs are set onto the chest will also affect the horse's action. If the setting of the legs is too broad, the horse will be a 'heavy' mover, if it is too narrow then there will be no heart room.

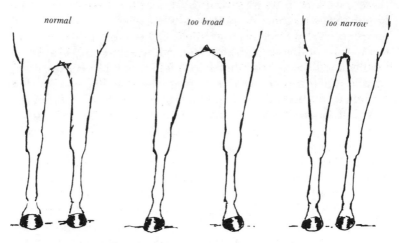

Conformation of the forelegs

The horse's legs and feet are the most important parts of its anatomy, as weak or malformed legs and feet will lead to problems of unsoundness and action and therefore loss of utility. Any deviation from the norm will lead to unnecessary stress on different joints and will render the horse unable to cope with the exertions being demanded of it. Good conformation will give

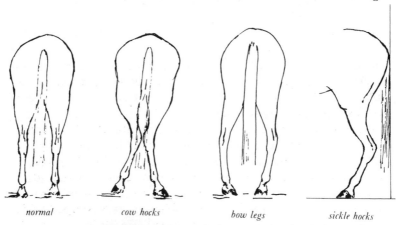

Conformation of the hind legs

him a fighting chance of achieving his potential. Cow hocks will make him move like a bovine, sickle hocks are weak hocks, and bow legs will give him a tendency to roll, like a ship in high seas; these are all undesirable in a racehorse.

Two other undesirable conditions are 'back at the knee' and 'over at the knee'. Being back at the knee is the worst of the two conditions because it puts more strain on the tendons and check ligaments that run down the back of the knee and leg. But you do not have to rule out a horse that seems slightly over at the knee, particularly if this fault is counterbalanced by nicely

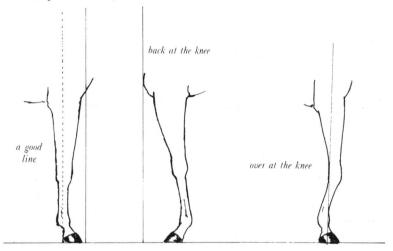

back at the knee

a good line

over at the knee

Straightness of leg

sloping pasterns. A horse that is 'tied in' below the knee has a cannon bone that lacks substance and is much narrower than the bone above the knee; it is a sign of possible weakness. Bone width from below the knee down to the fetlock should be the same all the way down.

Feet should be studied closely, especially the front feet, because it is essential that they are capable of cushioning the inevitable initial impact of half a ton of horse hitting the ground. They should be in proportion with the rest of the animal and all the same size (although it is normal for the back feet to be slightly smaller than the front feet). The frog (a V-shaped body on the sole of the foot) should be soft and well let down to provide grip and to help cushion impact. Sloping pasterns and shoulders also act as shock absorbers to reduce jarring of joints and allow a longer, lower stride. Long pasterns are prone to weakness, whereas short upright pasterns lead to jarring and consequent unsoundness. For maximum effectiveness, the pastern should be approximately 45 degrees from the perpendicular when the horse is standing square. Viewed from the side, a straight vertical line should pass from the centre of the elbow through the centre of the knee and pastern to the ground.

Look closely at the horse's legs. Lumps and bumps on the body are less worrying than those on the legs. If a yearling has signs of strain on his legs, such as spavins, windgalls and other unsightly bulges, then it proves that he is not even up to relaxing in a field, let alone racing.

The hips are an important fulcrum where the power generated from the back and quarters is transmitted through the hind legs and feet to the ground. Viewed from behind, the hips should be level. Uneven hips suggest an injury or weakness in conformation that cannot be ignored.

Look at the horse's shoes, if he has any on. Check whether they are equally worn down, or more worn on one foot, or on one side, than the other. If a horse favours one foot more, then the stress on the leg is increased. Also look for signs of brushing, over-reaching etc., as they too denote faulty action.

Joe Thomas, the late vice-President of the American Windfields Farm produced a check list of values for certain criteria to be examined when purchasing racehorses:

a) Overall appearance (size, presence, condition, bone etc.)   25 pts
b) Top line (head/neck/throat line, shoulder/ withers, back/croup/tail)   10 pts
c) Forelegs   35 pts
d) Hind legs   15 pts
e) Gait   15 pts

Total   100 pts

This list suggests that the most important aspect of anatomy is a good pair of front legs. Joe Thomas did not suggest that this was a foolproof guide to assessment, but it does help to concentrate the emphasis on the more important areas of the anatomy.

Michael Osborne, a leading veterinary surgeon in the Thoroughbred business, has compiled a list of vital statistics for the typical Northern Dancer type of racehorse:

Inside leg, 33 inches
Eye to tail, 88 inches
Shoulder to tail, 66 inches
Hock to ground, 24 inches
Hip to hock, 48 inches

Mr. Osborne has studied the Northern Dancer type in sufficient quantity to be able to produce this check list. This type of close-coupled, smaller Thoroughbred is being seen increasingly on courses now, especially in America, and Mr. Osborne predicts that this will be the recognisable shape of the Thoroughbred in years to come.

Computers are now being devised to facilitate the assessment of conformation. A horse is looked at through a view-finder and if the horse has good, balanced conformation a superimposed circle will touch the shoulder, wither, top of fetlock joint and point of haunch. Other assessment approaches will use similar criteria to fit the horse into a box shape rather than a circle. However, it is unlikely that such machines will replace the good horseman's eye, as too many other things must be taken into consideration when looking at horses. The top American trainer Wayne Lukas admits to sometimes buying a horse purely from the feeling it gives him as opposed to the way it fits into the ideal measurement scales.

The basic thing to remember is that, when studying conformation, you are looking for practicality of function, which just happens to be pleasing to the eye. Some producers of yearlings, especially in America, put so much condition on their animals, that the most the horse will be capable of is a waddle, and he will be three before he has lost enough flab to race, so be wary of glossy, rounded figures, however attractive they may seem at the time. Some horses will of course defy all the rules of conformation and will win on legs that would be more at home supporting a Georgian dining table. There is no guarantee that the best made horse will also be the fastest. I have heard self-confessed racing experts sniggering at a rather unlikely looking racehorse in the paddock, whose length of ear gave him a striking resemblance to Muffin the Mule. This ridiculed, lop-eared horse went on to win, despite comments that his ears would act as parachutes and increase wind resistance! Some trainers prefer horses with a big ear and large eye, regarding these as signs of genuineness.

Unfortunately, the horse world is littered with old wives' tales that may hamper you when it comes to choosing horses. For example, white legs are supposed to be weaker than black; chestnut mares are supposed to be too temperamental to be worth wasting time on (Pebbles and Unite are presumably exceptions). So do not let colours and markings put you off a good horse. Some people apparently gave one very flashy looking colt a wide berth at the sales some years ago. The flashy chestnut with the white face and legs turned out to be The Minstrel. There are also those horsemen who are a little wary of mares and fillies, regarding them as too unpredictable and moody, especially when they are in season. However, geldings and colts can also be unpredictable and no horse's good nature can be relied upon 100 per cent of the time. So avoid superstitions and apply logic.

4 Naming Your Horse

Naming the racehorse provides the owner with the opportunity to display his wit, knowledge of breeding, inability to spell, wicked penchant for tongue twisters or to promote his company. Care taken at this stage will reduce the likelihood of embarrassment later when your name is emblazoned on the racecard beneath the blush-provoking name of your horse, picked during a heavy merry-making session months ago. That name will be bellowed over the racecourse tannoy and transmitted into millions of homes via television and radio, so make sure you can live with it. Also bear in mind that the Thoroughbred is arguably the most beautiful and courageous of horses and deserves some respect and dignity. A racehorse may be forgiven for looking a little apologetic if he rejoices in the name of Mouldy Orange, or some other such abomination, that will elicit giggles from the irregular racegoers. These 'day out' punters often follow some pretty odd systems when selecting a horse to back, frequently singling one out purely because of its name, especially when they have no other information to go on.

As a rule, horses cannot be named and registered until they are yearlings, although, if you have a brilliant idea for your horse's name, it can be secured for you and reserved for up to twelve months in advance by submitting to Weatherby's the names of the sire and dam, plus a fee. If two owners request the same name for their horses, then the decision would be made by lot. Names must be limited to eighteen characters, which includes spaces, hence words in names being run together as in 'Lastofthebrownies' which looks awful, but sounds slightly better. Your choice of name should be accompanied by a veterinary surgeon's certificate of the horse's colour, age and markings and immediate breeding, i.e. the sire and dam. You may need to submit quite a few names before Weatherbys will accept one. Names may be rejected on the grounds that they are too similar to an already registered animal and may lead to confusion, and may also be refused if the animal is the product of artificial insemination, or of some other unnatural practice such as surrogate mothering. If the mare died after foaling, the use of a foster mother would not affect the naming of the orphaned foal.

Weatherbys produce, in book form, a list of registered names that may not be used. Some may become available in time, once the original name-holder is definitely no longer running, but there are names, especially marked, which are reserved for posterity; names such as Nijinsky, Sir Ivor, Brigadier Gerard and Arkle.

If you take a sudden dislike to your animal's name, then you can try to change it, but if the horse has been entered to race, it will be stuck with that name for the rest of its racing life.

Naming your horse after someone is only possible if you obtain that individual's permission in writing. Some people may feel honoured to have a racehorse named after them, but some may take offence, especially if the animal is useless or bears an uncanny resemblance in some part of its anatomy to its namesake! The name does not have to be in English, but the race commentators will thank you if it is not too difficult to pronounce.

Horses are frequently named to reflect their breeding, using the names of the sire and dam in obvious or more subtle ways to come up with a suitable title for the offspring, for example, a horse by Thatch out of Explosive is called Stubble Fire, linking the names of the parents in that of the offspring.

Horses named in anticipation of their earth shattering speed are ridiculed when they fail to show anything above second gear on the racecourse.

In the end, Weatherbys have the final say on what you call your horse, so you may have to submit a list of the names that you want or would agree to have, with no guarantee that your first choice will be accepted, or indeed that any of them will be. If you are lost for any ideas as to what to call the beast, Weatherbys may offer some suggestions.

Whatever you call the horse, the lad will abbreviate it or mutate it into something more manageable for every day life, like Sid, and that is the name that your horse will answer to, if anything.

5 Choosing Your Colours

The Jockey Club provides a list of colours and markings that it regards as acceptable and from which you should choose. A list of existing colours currently registered prevents you from duplicating someone else's colours which would lead to the most awful confusion for racing commentators as well as the general racing public.

The horse's owner or part-owners must register the colours on payment of a fee. Another fee has to be paid every twelve months thereafter to secure the colours for your future use.

To choose your colours, try to visualize a jockey on your horse, galloping out into the country, with your binoculars trained on the retreating duo. What colours could you pick up at that distance? Subtle shades and pastels are quite useless as they are colourless at that range. Dramatic colours are essential if you are to pick out your bay colt from the other twenty-four bay runners in a field. If you own a grey, then you can probably get by with wishy-washy colours because the horse itself will stand out in a crowd. As a rule, the more violently offensive the colours are close up, the more effective they are in terms of visibility. People will remember your colours even if they cannot remember your name, especially if you have succeeded in nauseating their eyeballs!

Markings include stripes, epaulets, braces, crossbelts, hoops, spots, the cross of Lorraine etc. and can all be quite striking and identifiable at some distance, particularly on a plain background. It is impossible to get single colours now, as they were snapped up years ago by the old families who have been in racing for generations. You will have to make do with the colour choices that are left. The markings can be displayed on the hat silks and sleeves as well as the main body.

If you have more than one horse and you are running two in

Some examples of racing silks

the same race, e.g. a pacemaker and a real contender, then there will have to be slight differences in the colours carried by one of your horses to aid identification, e.g. a different cap colour. Such changes should be declared at Scale before the race. The public will immediately assume that the horse wearing your first colours will be the one with a chance, and this will usually be reflected in the betting, even though you and your trainer may find it difficult to choose between your two runners.

Some trainers use an easily identifiable piece of tack on their horses to aid recognition during a race, such as sheepskin nosebands or light coloured breast plates.

If you run your horse without registering your colours, then you are committing an offence under the Rules of Racing and will be fined. Jockeys are used to looking kaleidoscopic, so do not be overly concerned that your choice will clash with the stable jockey's hair. He will not turn down the ride on those grounds!

6 Vaccination

A horse to be raced under the Rules of Racing must have an up to date vaccination certificate to be available to Stewards, veterinary surgeons etc., should they require to see it. Failure to have vaccinated your horse is irresponsible and, if discovered, may result in non-admittance to racecourses and maybe a fine as well. The racecourse checks on certificates are random and one has to hope that all other horses have been given the same strict vaccination programme as yours. Thus there is no 100 per cent check and the responsibility lies with the horse's connections.

The vaccination that people are mostly concerned with is the equine anti-influenza vaccination, although your horse can and should be vaccinated against many other potential health hazards such as tetanus. The risk of infection on a racecourse is great because your animal will be mixing with many others from all over the country, and maybe some from abroad as well. An epidemic could bring racing to a standstill, and, consequently, calamitous effects on the racing industry. Recent surveys have shown a deplorable lack of hygiene in some racecourse stables. It is here that your horse will be most at risk as he may only have the unchanged straw bedding of the previous occupant to stand and lie on. Time does not always allow for the lad to disinfect the stable before the next horse arrives and hence the very real risk of infection.

A racehorse should not receive an injection if he is due to race in up to ten days' time, as he will need a little time to rest and get his strength back. Thus injections should really be administered before the horse is due to start his racing season. The delay between the vaccination and racing also allows time for the injections to integrate with the bloodstream and become fully operative.

Strictly speaking, your trainer should see to your horse's

54

vaccination programme, but if he forgets or, for some other reason, omits to carry out the correct vaccinations, then it will be you who misses out on the racing side of racehorse ownership.

Your horse's passport, provided by Weatherbys, should display the fact that the two primary injections have been performed 21, or up to 92, days apart.

Foals should receive their first booster jabs between 150 and 215 days after the second of the primary injections. Subsequent boosters should be administered at annual intervals, after the 150 to 215 day booster.

This vaccination programme should be displayed on the horse's passport and certified by a veterinary surgeon.

If you hear a horse at the stables coughing, or see a discharge trickling from its nose, then draw your trainer's attention to it. He will no doubt know all about it, as it is the lad's job to monitor such changes in his charge, but it pays to make sure that such things are under control, otherwise your horse might be at risk. The trainer should have an isolation box to prevent the spread of any unpleasant and unwelcome germs throughout the yard. The box should be well away from the main yard and the equine patient should not share a grooming kit, feed bowl, rugs, bandages or water bucket with any other horse unless those articles have been disinfected before and after use. It is all too easy to be lax in a busy stable, especially where lads are in charge of three or four horses at a time. In larger establishments, several isolation boxes will be necessary.

If the trainer does not act quickly in the advent of signs of viral infection, then he may become one of those unfortunate trainers whose entire stable goes down with the dreaded virus, and misses the season's racing in consequence. If this happens, try to be patient and support your trainer, providing he took all possible precautions to avoid it, and he undoubtedly did, as only a fool would treat his own livelihood with such disregard. It is usually pure bad luck, and no amount of injections would have prevented it. The virus still remains one of the mysteries of modern science (as does the equivalent human flu) but the Equine Research Station is working on improving the treatments and vaccinations available.

When the stable does seem to be picking up, do not hurry your trainer into running your horse before the close of the season.

The virus still remains one of the mysteries . . .

Working a horse that is still under the influence of a virus is risking more damage to the animal's respiratory tract than the virus itself would do and may lead to irreparable damage.

Moving your horse to another yard during this crisis is not necessarily a good idea either, as the virus may be dormant in your animal, even though he shows no sign of illness at the time. It may manifest itself later in the new yard and will make you the most unpopular person there. A trainer who suspects that you are taking your horse out of a 'sick' stable will be wise to refuse admittance to his.

As with any patient, show the horse a little sympathy and consideration and leave him to the care of his lad.

7 Jockeys and Jockeys' Riding Fees

It will come as no surprise to hear that National Hunt jockey fees are set higher than those of their Flat-race riding colleagues, presumably to incorporate danger money owing to the added risks involved in their profession. The fees are reviewed annually between the two representative bodies of the groups involved, these being the Racehorse Owners' Association (R.O.A.) and the Jockeys' Association of Great Britain. If these discussions make no progress and stalemate is reached, then the Stewards of the Jockey Club may be called in to dab fevered brows and to determine the rate to be paid, thus acting as mediators when required.

The Jockeys' Association of Great Britain is obviously concerned that some of their less successful jockeys are living on a pittance if they cannot collect enough rides and are obliged to try to find other work to keep them and their families going. The Racehorse Owners' Association negotiates to ensure that jockeys do not price themselves out of the market by expecting an increase each year.

Obviously, the jockey's income is linked to the number of rides he can obtain, with the addition of a percentage of the prize money if he rides a winner. When the top Flat jockeys ride a horse to a win in one of the Classics, they can, once the horse has retired to stud, claim a share of the fees. Lester Piggott was a keen advocate of this arrangement.

Good jockeys tend to get the good rides, but it is difficult for a jockey to prove his worth to the world if he cannot get any decent rides. These jockeys are in a classic Catch-22 situation where they will only be noticed if they ride a winner, but they do not get a chance to ride such horses until they have proved themselves. To a certain extent, as in stallion selection, the choice of a jockey may be governed by which rider is 'in vogue'

57

at the time. A popular jockey may find himself riding at two meetings in a single day, leading to panic if he is held up in traffic, so it may be more convenient to use a jockey who is working all day at the course where your horse will run, rather than holding out for a big name.

The jockey fee is usually subject to V.A.T. with a percentage based on the jockey fee to be paid into the Professional Riders Insurance Scheme. However not all jockeys are V.A.T. registered. At present the percentage stands at 10 per cent for Flat-race jockeys and $12\frac{1}{2}$ per cent for National Hunt jockeys who are probably more likely to get injured and require its services. The Professional Riders Insurance Scheme is available to jockeys injured in their work, either on the racecourse or riding work on the gallops. In addition to this, there exists a registered charity called the Injured Jockeys' Fund which acts in a similar way, but relies on donations from the public. They produce Christmas cards and calendars to sell to raise money, the cards being very popular with the racing fraternity who give them and receive them with predictable regularity.

Both these organizations are invaluable when one considers the sort of insurance policies for which a jockey would not be considered. The obligatory hours on the road adds to the risk in a jockey's everyday life. Window cleaning and jockeying are two trades that insurance men shun, or offer ridiculously high rates to.

Apprentice and conditional jockeys are no cheaper to employ, but they have to halve the earnings with their trainer who is responsible for the expenses incurred. These jockeys are learning the trade and will be eternally grateful if you agree to let them ride your horse in a race. All the champion jockeys had to start this way, and the trainer will be sure to tell you if he thinks his pupil is not up to it yet. Some horses run better for inexperienced riders, taking care of their young jockeys and welcoming the slightly gentler handling they may receive, as opposed to the stronger urging tactics of the experienced jockeys. However a bad apprentice can put your horse right back in his training, especially if the lad has rough hands which may cause severe damage to the horse's mouth. This is particularly likely with young Flat racehorses who still have very soft skin and lips which tear very easily if abused. It takes a very short time to ruin a horse's mouth and a lot more time and patience to regain his confidence. Horses that pull during a race may be keen or may be running frightened of the bit in their mouths which has hurt them before. As the jockey pulls on the bit trying to steady the pulling horse the animal's worst fears are confirmed as his mouth is tugged at. Horses are illogical when it comes to fearing the bit as they will grab it and hold it rather than pulling back from it. So be sure that you trust a youngster on your horse, whilst remembering that they all need the chance to prove themselves.

A good working relationship with your jockey will pay dividends when you want an in-depth break-down of how your horse ran. The jockey is the only man who actually experiences first hand the way your horse runs in a race, so he is the ultimate source of information. He can help a 'green' or inexperienced horse to win by sympathetic handling, or can urge an old hand to make the effort that the rider knows the horse is capable of. The jockey must be able to assess a horse immediately, sometimes riding the horse for the very first time actually on the racecourse.

Large stables retain jockeys for their owners' personal use and these owners will pay a retaining fee. If your trainer has no retained jockey, then the best jockey available will be employed to ride your horse. A retained stable jockey will be automatically engaged to ride your horse if he is the correct weight. If, however, there is another runner from the stable in the same race, the jockey may choose the horse that he feels has the best chance.

The jockey can assess your horse in the actual race and may come back from the race with some suggestions, e.g. to run the horse on different going, over a shorter/longer distance, with/without blinkers/visors, etc. Some jockeys may give a favourable opinion of the horse to please the owner and keep the ride, but withhold their real opinion.

A good jockey will make all the difference between being first or an 'also ran' and as such his skill should be valued highly.

8 Types of Race

There are two main divisions for racing under rules, these being the Flat and National Hunt racing. Within National Hunt racing exist two further subdivisions; hurdling and steeple-chasing. Further subdivisions for types of race include selling, claiming, handicap, maiden, novice, auction and hunterchase races and more.

Flat Racing

This needs little introduction. It is the oldest form of racing, dating back to the years B.C. when men tested their horses without the added interruption of obstacles to the extended stride. Flat races are normally run over shorter distances than the National Hunt races, ranging from the short sprinting bursts of five furlongs, up to two miles and beyond for three-year-olds and above. Flat races are started out of stalls to ensure a more even break, which can be crucial, as yards lost at the start of a race may never be made up, especially over the shorter sprinting distances. The Flat is the money earner of the two types of racing, not just in higher prize money, but in later stud and broodmare value.

The five Classics (the 1000 Guineas, 2000 Guineas, Derby, Oaks and St. Leger) are designed to pit the top three-year-olds against each other over varying distances and courses. You know that you have arrived as an owner when you can enter a horse with a chance in one of these prestigious races. Most of us will own 'also rans' in lesser races, battling for the sort of prize money that would not even cover the entry fee to one of the Classic races.

Flat racehorses can be fitted into four categories, although horses can and do run over two or three of the distances described, so the divisions are not definitive.

Horses that race best over five furlongs to seven furlongs are referred to as sprinters, as races over such distances are pure speed races.

The horses that race over seven furlongs to one and a quarter miles successfully are called middle-distance horses. Races over distances of one and a quarter to one and a half miles require speed and stamina, and lastly, one and a half to two mile races and beyond are for stayers.

Tesio, the talented Italian racehorse owner, breeder and trainer suggested that a great horse can only be produced from Classic standard relatives going back to the fifth generation, winning over one mile and up to two miles. The current trend is for the top stayers to be less popular at stud than the faster horses. In his book *Breeding the Racehorse*, Tesio sums up his principle of assessing the ability of a Flat racehorse thus: 'Speed over a long period of time means staying power, but staying power over a short period of time never means speed'.

The problem is to isolate the ideal distance(s) for your horse, which may change as the horse matures. This may require some experimental runs until the horse shows where its ability really lies. The champion sprinter Ajdal is an example of a horse that was disappointing until his correct trip was isolated.

The Flat season runs for eight months, from the end of March to the start of November, although with the possible advent of all-weather tracks, there may be no true end to the season because these surfaces can provide the desirable going throughout the year. The all-weather track may produce 'surface specialists' in our future racehorses, where a horse acts better on the artificial going than on the turf which will be an interesting development in British racing. It is already the case in America where they have the choice of the turf or the dirt tracks. The man-made surfaces are being tested for their suitability for National Hunt racing as well.

Owners of backward two-year-olds should welcome these tracks if they prove to provide consistent going as they can give their youngsters more time to mature before racing them at the end of the year to ascertain their merits and to see if it is worth persevering with the horse as a three-year-old. In this way, the owner will be able to save himself the expense of keeping a poor racehorse in training and can start looking for a replacement for the future.

Hurdling

Hurdling can be a means to an end, or a stepping stone to steeplechasing. Hurdlers are more numerous than steeplechasers, hence it is often more difficult to succeed in placing a hurdler to win than a steeplechaser. A hurdler can treat the obstacles he faces with a little more contempt than a steeplechaser, whose fences are unyielding. Hurdles are constructed to be inviting to the horse (if not the jockey) by sloping away from the animal as it approaches, thus assisting judgement of the take-off. A hurdle will collapse if knocked, a fence will not but will tend to bring down the assaulter. A horse that jumps economically can gain ground over obstacles and conserve energy for the final finishing effort. A clumsy jumper has no future over hurdles or fences. Hurdle races are run a little faster than steeplechases as a rule. There are no penalties for knocking down a hurdle, just as in human hurdling. Hitting the hurdle is only a disadvantage in that it will result in loss of impetus and balance. You can still win if you demolish the lot, as long as you finish in front. Only the hurdle builder will criticize you. There must not be fewer than six flights of hurdles to jump in the first one and a half miles, and subsequently one flight every quarter mile. The minimum distance is 2 miles.

Steeplechasing

Steeplechasing is a sport for the brave of heart and horses who are sound in wind and limb. The horses also have to be good jumpers, or they risk turning over if they meet a fence incorrectly. The best horses will frequent the big Cheltenham Festival meeting in March and the Aintree meeting for the Grand National, a race notorious throughout the civilized world. Only the best horses should be confronted with fences like Becher's Brook and the Chair, and it is regrettable that some owners will risk their lower class animals over the course just for the prestige of it. Where is the prestige in causing a favourite to fall as your horse has apoplexy at the first fence? Perhaps the conditions of this race could be made more stringent to ensure that only those capable are entered. The best horses are often saved from this test in the hope that they will avoid unnecessary

Steeplechasing is a sport for the brave . . .

injury. Arkle, for example, was saved for other National Hunt conquests.

The National Hunt season is longer than that of the Flat, beginning in the first week of August and closing at the end of May. In steeplechase races there must be no fewer than twelve fences in the first two miles, and at least six in each subsequent mile, with one open ditch per mile and, up until recently, one water jump, but the latter is now optional, the Ayr racecourse being one of the first to have its water jump removed. No steeplechase can be shorter than two miles.

This has given a brief introduction to the two codes (types) of racing. To simplify matters, Flat racing can be divided into the following main types of race:

Nursery races
Maiden races
Claiming races
Selling races

Apprentice/amateur races
Handicaps
Pattern races
Auction races
Sweepstakes

National Hunt racing can be divided in a similar fashion:

Hurdle races (handicap and non-handicap)
Steeplechase (handicap and non-handicap)
Claiming races
Selling races
Amateur races
Novice hurdle/chase races
Hunterchases
Bumpers
Conditions races

Flat Races

NURSERY HANDICAPS These races are restricted to two-year-olds who carry a top weight of 9st 7lb, and a minimum weight of not less than 7st 7lb, but these races are not run before July 1st to give the young horse some time to mature.

MAIDEN RACES These are designed for the horse that has not won a race, however it is important to read the small print when entering a horse as there are two types of maiden race in existence, the 'maidens at starting' and the 'maidens at closing'.

Nursery races

In the former, all horses are truly maidens i.e. non-winners. In the latter, a horse may have won a race in the interim period between entering and actually competing. Colts will be maidens at the start of their career as well as fillies despite the feminine term. Maiden races are probably some of the most exciting, as the owner will actually get to see his horse and his colours making their debut on the racecourse. It brings a lump to the throat and you will feel your heart drop through your diaphragm in your anticipation and anxiety. The jockeys find it exciting too, as they wrestle and coax and curse unruly youngsters into the stalls, hoping they will agree to emerge on the other side when the time comes to race. Older horses are still called maidens if they have not won a race.

In maiden races on the Flat and over hurdles, over-subscribed races can be divided to cope with the number of entries at the declaration stage. In hurdle races, the numbers of horses involved has meant that the horses that have the most unplaced runs will be the first to face elimination. Therefore, possession of an unsuccessful hurdler can be the same as having no racehorse at all, if he never gets beyond the declaration stage.

CLAIMING RACES If a horse is claimed out of a claiming race, then the owner will receive the claiming price, as published, less 10 per cent to the racecourse, plus 15 per cent of any extra above the claiming price. This can be a lucrative time for the race-course, but it can also be a demoralising time for the owner, who has to lose his horse or spend out more to get a replacement for his claimed horse, or buy his own back, even though he has set the claiming price of his horse with the trainer beforehand. The claiming price is usually higher than one would expect to pay for the same horse at auction.

To claim a horse, the claim should be made in writing, signed, sealed and delivered to the Clerk of the Scales within ten minutes of the 'all right' signal being displayed on the number board. Once submitted the claim may not be withdrawn or changed. In the case of two equal claims being made, the decision may be made by lot.

Owners, friends of owners and wives and husbands of owners could not, at one time, claim the horse back for its original owner, nor could the horse be returned to the stable from which it had been bought, but this Rule – 97 part (iii) – was altered in March 1988 to allow the owner to claim his horse. Claiming the horse back costs the owner 10 per cent of the published claiming price and 85 per cent over that price.

Only one claim is permitted per person, per horse, or the claimant can be reported to the Stewards. However, one claim can be made for several runners in the same race by the same person. The sale must be sealed by payment, or settled to the Clerk of the Scale's satisfaction within half an hour of the 'all right' signal. In the event that the price is not paid, the claimant becomes guilty of an offence under the Rules of Racing and loses his claim, and the horse will go to the next highest claimant whose payment should be secured with the Clerk of the Scales within forty-five minutes of the 'all right' signal being displayed. At present claims in Britain are made after the race, in the United States the claims are made before the race is run.

So why do owners run their horses in claiming races and risk losing them? The idea of the claiming race is that the weight allotted to the horse in the race is linked to the claiming price fixed before the race. Thus claiming races provide the horse with an opportunity to win a race, whereas non-claiming races would see the horse harshly handicapped, with his chance of success possibly removed. The problem is to decide what weight would give the horse a winning chance without risking the horse being undersold. In numerical terms, if 9st 7lb is the standard weight, and the claiming price is a minimum of £15,000, then £1,000 will be removed from the horse's price for each pound less in weight that it carries. Claiming a horse provides the new owner with an instant racehorse, fit and ready to race again in the near future.

The claiming race is also a good battle ground for the shrewd trainer who can assess his horse and its competitors literally pound for pound. If he puts the price too high, then the horse's extra weight will ensure that you lose the race and keep the horse. The official handicapper probably would have allotted him a similar weight in a handicap. If the weight is too low, then the horse will win by a distance and be sold for nothing near his real value. If trainers judge it correctly, a competitive race should ensue. It gives the trainer his only chance to play handicapper to his own horse.

SELLING RACES If you enter a horse in a selling race over jumps or on the Flat, and it wins, then your horse will be put up for auction to the highest bidder, which could be you if you wanted to buy the horse back in. This can be a very expensive way to keep a horse in training, but if he is a lower class horse this may be all that he is capable of winning. There is no need to feel less proud of the animal if he wins in this sort of company, as long as he wins. If he does not win, he can still be claimed. The selling race is a good medium for getting rid of inferior animals, but remember that the owner will not receive all of the selling price attained.

The owner receives the race prize money, the advertised selling price of the horse and, at present, 20 per cent of any extra above the selling price up to £2,000, 25 per cent of anything above £2,000 up to £3,000, and 50 per cent of any extra above £3,000. The other percentage of the profit of the sale goes to the racecourse.

The bidding must be started at the amount of the guaranteed prize money up to £2,000. If the guaranteed prize money is higher, then the bidding must be started at £2,000 upwards. If a non-winner in a selling race is claimed, then the owner will receive the pre-published claiming price plus 15 per cent of anything above this price. Again, the racecourse receives the remainder.

If your horse is entered for a claiming or selling race, then your trainer should warn you that the horse may well be sold. He may assume that you know what these races are, so make sure that you do, or you risk losing your horse just as you are celebrating its first win.

APPRENTICE/AMATEUR RACES Apprentice races are open to apprentice jockeys only and not to professionals. Where apprentices ride against professionals, they can claim a weight allowance, usually in handicap and selling races and races below a certain value. If the race is above this prize money sum, then the apprentice will ride on equal terms with the professionals, unable to claim his allowance.

The allowances on the Flat for apprentices are determined by the apprentice's number of winning rides. He may claim 7lb until he has won ten races under Rules, 5lb until he has won 50 races and 3lb until he has steered 75 winners home.

Amateur riders' races are closed to professionals and the weights are set higher for amateur Flat races enabling the amateur riders to follow a less strict dieting and wasting regime than that employed by the professional jockey.

HANDICAPS Horses that run in handicaps have had their ability assessed by the Official Handicapper for the Jockey Club, usually after three runs, and a grade allotted which can then be used to determine the weight the horse will carry in a handicap race. The horses are rated in four groups, these being the 0–75 group, the 0–90 group, the 0–100 and the 0–115 group. If the horse allotted the top weight in a race is withdrawn, then the next highest handicapped horse will have to carry top weight. The better a horse runs in handicaps, the more the handicapper will penalize him by weighting him down until he does fail. It must be a demoralizing experience for a genuine trier, but is a good test of the limits of the animal's ability. If the weights get too great, the next step would be to take the horse out of handicaps and perhaps move up to Listed or Group races.

In handicap races, the entries may exceed the safety factor for the number of horses allowed to run at one time, so the horses that carry the lowest weights will be eliminated. Elimination in non-handicap races is by ballot. It is possible to have your horse balloted out regularly and can lead to immense frustration for owner, trainer and lad, who have the horse fit and ready to run; a real case of 'all dressed up and nowhere to go'. To get trapped in this way may force the owner to sell that animal and try again with another.

National Hunt horses also have rate-restricted handicaps. Some trainers place their horses to get them well handicapped after a few defeats, to go on and land a successful gamble in poorer company or over a different distance. The Stewards will note such a horse's exploits with interest and may require the trainer to elaborate on his opinion of the horse!

The Long Handicap is a list of racing weights, which are assessed purely on a horse's ability before it has raced. If, once a horse has been declared to run, its allotted weight is less than the minimum level for a particular handicap race, the weight will then be increased to the minimum level thus effectively adding a penalty to the horse.

Pre-sale inspection at Tattersalls Highflyer sales.

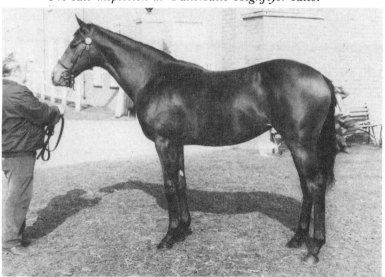

A yearling filly at the croup-higher-than-withers period of growth. She lacks depth of girth, is still rather leggy, a little tucked in below the knee, and has long cannon bones and upright shoulders.

A yearling filly with a good body and 'clean' legs. She is strong over the loins, has a promising outline, an 'honest' head, and seems well balanced but rather small.

A yearling colt with early muscle development which makes him seem much more mature than his contemporaries. He has a lovely sloping shoulder which should counterbalance his slightly upright pasterns.

A Tattersalls auctioneer extracting one more bid from buyers.

Two of trainer David Thom's horses working on the Al-Bahathri all-weather gallop at Newmarket.

Trainer James Bennett supervises the schooling of one of his steeple-chasers.

Owners and trainers in the paddock at Pontefract racecourse.

Horses are reassessed regularly for the purpose of handicapping, and, if a horse wins before being assessed again, it will have to carry a penalty, determined by the ease of its win, unless otherwise stipulated in the conditions of the race. The conditions of such races may penalise horses that have won a certain amount of money with a specific penalty. Two-year-old fillies will claim a 5lb allowance in races against colts, i.e. the fillies will carry 5lb less, and the three-year-old fillies claim 3lb. This is called a sex allowance, which is allotted on the assumption that fillies at that age will not be as strong and forward as colts of the same age, thus attempting to give the fillies' an equal chance.

National Hunt handicaps give the top-weighted horse not less than 12st, and the bottom weight not less than 10st, although the handicapper may lower the minimum weight at his discretion.

PATTERN RACES are the most prestigious of all Flat races, and are chosen to provide the best conditions to test top class horses of all ages throughout the Flat season. The prize money for Pattern races is well above the average. These races are reviewed each year by the European Pattern Race Committee represented by the U.K., Ireland, Italy, West Germany and France. Weatherbys produce a book listing the European Pattern race conditions for each year. There are three types of Pattern race; Group One races are the championship races, including the Classics. The English Classics are open to three-year-olds only and consist of:

The 1000 Guineas – run over a mile at Newmarket in May and restricted to fillies.

The 2000 Guineas – also run over a mile at Newmarket two days after the fillies' Classic and is open to both sexes.

The Derby – regarded as the most prestigious Classic, run over one and a half miles at Epsom and invariably leading to an immense increase in the value of the winner, plus the subsequent high stud fees when the horse retires, usually at the end of the season. Both sexes are entitled to run.

The Oaks – run over one and a half miles at Epsom, and restricted to fillies.

The St. Leger – the oldest of all the Classics, having first been run in 1776, over one mile, six furlongs and 120 yards at Doncaster, open to both sexes. (A furlong is equal to 220 yards or one eighth of a mile.)

Fillies running in the 2000 Guineas and Derby can claim 5lb, (i.e. carry 5lb less) but can only claim 3lb in the St. Leger.

The owner of a Classic or Pattern race winner will receive less than half (currently 46.4 per cent) of the prize money. Other claimants to the prize money are the trainer, who takes 5.7 per cent, the jockey, 4.06 per cent, and the stable, 3 per cent. The money won by placed horses is also broken down in this way. Full details of the allocation of prize money are in Rule 194 of the Rules of Racing.

Group Two races are rated just below Group One standard and produce some very useful horses, Group Three races are of the lowest standard and are mainly of domestic interest, but are, nevertheless, more than respectable races. Pattern races may be referred to as Graded Stakes races. Listed races come just below Group Three races in standard.

Weight for age is the only differential in defining weights to be carried in Group One races. Group Two and Three races penalize winners of Group One races if such horses are entered to run in lower company.

AUCTION RACES These races are restricted to horses bought at public auction in Great Britain or Ireland for less than an expressed sum, and are usually for two-year-olds, 'maidens at starting' whose weights are governed by the price they fetched at auction.

SWEEPSTAKES These are races where the entrance fee and subscription i.e. forfeit (declaration fee) goes to the winner and all the placed horses. Guaranteed Sweepstake races are funded by the owners paying entry and declaration fees, reducing the amount to be found by the racecourse itself. These races are in the low prize money bracket.

National Hunt Races

Hurdle races, steeplechases, claiming races and selling races have been discussed previously, but there are five more categories of National Hunt Races.

AMATEUR RACES National Hunt amateur riders under 25 years of age holding a conditional jockey's licence or a 'category

B' amateur rider's permit can claim their allowance in all races except those restricted to conditional jockeys.

Amateur National Hunt jockeys can use their status to gain experience before turning professional. Some amateurs go right to the top, as did well-known jockeys Peter Scudamore and Richard Dunwoody.

NOVICE HURDLES AND STEEPLECHASES The novice hurdler and steeplechaser are equally stimulating rides for the National Hunt jockeys who really earn their fee, risking life and limb on a horse that may be so surprised by the experience of racing that he may forget to pick up his feet over the obstacles. Novice hurdlers and steeplechasers are horses that have not won a race at the start of the season. When a horse has won, it can still race as a novice for the rest of the season.

HUNTERCHASES If you own a horse that has hunted with hounds and you have a hunter's certificate from the huntsman to attest to this fact, then you may enjoy sending the animal hunterchasing, in which case you must register his name and submit the hunter's certificate to Weatherbys. Horses that have raced between November 1st and January 31st will *not* be entitled to race for the hunterchase season commencing February 1st. As with all racehorses, your hunterchaser will require a horse passport which the Clerk of the Course may wish to see. You will receive the passport when the horse is registered. A passport is the identity document for racehorses, recording markings for identification purposes and is issued by the Stewards of the Jockey Club when the horse is fully registered. It is issued to named two-year-olds upwards.

The hunterchase jockey is an amateur and can be the owner of the horse he accompanies around the course, adding that extra element of excitement to racehorse ownership by fulfilling the dream of the capable owner/rider. One hopes that the owner/rider takes this sport seriously, and acquires the necessary skill to reduce the threat he poses to the safety of his opponents and, not least, to himself. A book on National Hunt race-riding technique has been written by John Hislop entitled *Steeplechasing* (J. A. Allen & Co.) which might be of use to budding race riders.

BUMPERS These are National Hunt Flat races. Bumpers are confined to amateur and claiming riders. The horses must not have raced under Rules before and should be aged between four and six years in January, and five and seven years after January 1st which marks the official birthday for all Thoroughbred horses regardless of their actual birthdates. It is therefore useful, especially when buying for the Flat, to acquire an early foal rather than a late one, as the latter may lose six months of development and maturation to his opponents which he would have to be very good indeed to overcome. Horses can only compete in bumpers five times, after which they become ineligible. The purpose of these races is to give horses that appear to have a bright future over fences experience on the racecourse.

A more extreme example of this type of race exists in Ireland where racecourses allow Schooling Hurdle races, under no Rules, with no betting and the winner is of little importance. Hurdles may be missed out and avoided if so desired. Thus these races are purely schooling exercises for young, 'rusty' or sour horses.

CONDITIONS RACES can be Listed or lesser class races. They exist for both codes of racing and are literally any race where specific conditions apply to entry. Unlike ordinary handicap races, the weights to be carried in conditions races are calculated upon the number and type of races won, or upon the amount of prize money won. Once the conditions for these races have been made, the handicapper has no power to change them.

Weight For Age

Weight for age is the rule imposed in races where young horses race against their elders, and applies to any race which is not a handicap or a seller. Older horses have matured in strength and structure by the time they are six years old and can carry more weight than a three-year-old. A scale of weight for age, invented by Admiral Rous, which changes throughout the season, is produced for easy reference in several publications including the *Raceform* and *Programme of Meetings*.

Entry Rules

When entering a horse for a race, the conditions of entry, entry cost and declaration fee will be set out in the *Racing Calendar* and in the *Programme of Meetings* discussed later, and so there is no excuse for entering a horse in a race for which he is not eligible. The Rules state – Rule 124(V) – 'Trainers are responsible for ensuring that they do not declare horses to run in any races for which they are not qualified under the conditions of the races and these rules'.

Entering a horse that is not qualified would lead to the owner losing his entry fee. So know your races and leave the entries to your trainer until you know exactly what you are doing.

9 A Day at the Races

As a rule, the trainer will run your stable road-show himself when your horse, or horses, are racing, and you will be free to enjoy yourself and entertain friends whilst calming the nerves with alcohol. However, you may not be able to watch the racing at your leisure at every meeting.

. . . free to enjoy yourself . . .

In the normal course of events, you will collect your owner's badge to gain free admittance and proceed to relax in the members' enclosure until the day's racing swings into action.

The difference in entry price to the various divisions open to the racegoer at the racecourse is sometimes not reflected by the difference in amenities. In some cases, an owner's badge will only seem to entitle you to a shorter walk to the paddock and a higher class of toilet facilities. On the other hand, some courses will provide reserved areas for owners and their trainers to view the racing from a good vantage point. When one considers that racing would not exist without the people who own the horses, it is surprising that they do not universally receive a better welcome at the racecourses.

On occasion, however, your trainer may be attending a different meeting, and the travelling head lad another, leaving you with the most responsible member of the staff that is not already employed elsewhere. If this is the case, then you may find yourself in charge of the day's operation, assuming you are still intent on running the horse at this event without its usual back-up team.

First of all, you must get the trainer to make out and sign the declaration form. You must declare your horse a runner at the weighing room at least three-quarters of an hour before the race. You may find it helpful to have a friend with you as well as the member of stable staff who should both be given the Authority to Act, as discussed earlier, so that more people are available in case of a Stewards' enquiry, objection, collection of trophy, etc.

You should read the entry for your horse in the official race-card carefully to ensure that it is accurate, i.e. your colours are described correctly, the horse's age and colour is correct etc. If you fail to notice an error then you may be fined for not complying with the details, even though it is the course and/or Weatherbys who are incorrect.

If you position yourself at the weighing room, then you will see when your jockey arrives. If he is very late or injured in a previous race, then engage another jockey and advise the Stewards' secretary, or if time does not permit, then tell the Clerk of the Course or the Clerk of the Scales, whichever you find first. You are entitled to enter the first door of the weighing room as the owner of a runner, but must ask an assistant to find the jockey for you.

It will be wiser to let the stable lad or your other assistant saddle up your runner, as the racecourse is no place to learn how to do it, and the jockey will curse you if the saddle is not secured properly and safely. Faulty or badly adjusted tack can risk a jockey's life, as well as possibly damaging your horse.

Once the horse is saddled, meet the horse and jockey in the

. . . ask an assistant to find the jockey . . .

paddock as usual. It is probably best if you do not give any riding instructions to the jockey unless you really know what you are doing. The trainer will have discussed the horse with the jockey before so your directions will be a little superfluous. Wishing the jockey luck will do.

. . . do not give any riding instructions to the jockey

After the race, make sure that the jockey weighs in as soon as possible if he was in the frame (i.e. placed). If an apprentice was riding for you, then, in the event of a Stewards' Enquiry, either you or the trainer's representative would have to accompany him to appear before the Stewards.

In the event of an objection, a red flag will be raised if the winner is being objected to, or a red and white flag for a placed horse. An objection can be made to the Clerk of the Scales if you believe your horse was hampered in his bid to win by bumping, boring and crossing or some other form of interference such as taking another horse's ground. The objection can be lodged by the owner, trainer, or jockey, and should be accompanied by a deposit which will be returned if the Stewards agree with you. Objections must be lodged before the winner has weighed in. If the objection is upheld, then the Stewards will rearrange the frame, either putting the horse down a place, last or disqualifying him.

If your objection is overruled then you may lose your deposit. If the objection is regarded as being 'frivolous' then the objector may be fined a sum in excess of his initial deposit. If one of the Stewards himself sees reason to object, then no payment is made. Once made, objections may not be withdrawn unless the Stewards permit it.

In the event of losing their objection owners, trainers and jockeys have the right to appeal against the Stewards' decision to the Stewards of the Jockey Club within seven days of the episode. Another deposit is needed with the Notice of Appeal. The Stewards of the Jockey Club may then confirm or overrule the Course Stewards' original decision, and the horse may be given back his race and the owner his prize money.

Your day at the races can be made slightly less expensive if the travel costs can be shared amongst the owners if several horses from the stable are racing at the same meeting. This can be organised with your trainer. Travelling expenses may be one of the factors that will prevent your horse racing at some of the more distant tracks where he may have a better chance of winning. The pros and cons have to be weighed up when deciding on which courses to run the horse. If the horse is only capable of winning if it has to travel to what the owner regards as the end of the earth, then he may consider selling and buying another horse, with, hopefully, more chance of local success. Alternatively, the horse could be trained nearer to the easier courses to cut down on travelling expenses.

As with people, some horses are not good travellers but are physically unable to be sick, so they probably feel even worse than a human would in the same situation. Such nervous travellers can work themselves up into quite a state by the time they reach their destination and are then unlikely to show their true ability on the racecourse. In this case, you may be obliged to cast your net closer to home.

Some horses go better on courses with particular character-istics such as right- or left-handed courses, tight-turning courses or long straights, undulating or level surfaces, and the trainer should be able to assess this when placing his runners. One-course specialists show a singular dislike for anything but their favourite course, and may lose all form when raced elsewhere.

The variety of English racecourses enables most horses to find at least one that suits them, but it may entail a lot of travel expenditure until you find the right sort of course. However, the talented racehorse will be tested in his ability to handle many different courses. Consistency in performance is one of the goals in racing horses, and a horse that has to be pandered to to the extent that you are literally limited to one or two courses can never be regarded as a good racehorse, whether he wins at these two courses or not.

Remember that at the end of the day's racing the lad, once he has driven the box home, has to see your horse settled comfort-ably before he can relax himself. A token of your esteem would make the long haul back to the stables slightly less of a chore and will ensure his feeling of satisfaction for a job well done.

10 If Things Go Wrong

Things have not necessarily gone wrong if, at the close of the season, your horse has not won a race. If you cannot afford to be patient and see if it will train on, then you might want to sell it and try again with a new prospect. Indeed your trainer may advise you to do this if he can see no potential in the animal after having worked with it for the past year.

If you cannot afford to be patient . . .

Racing is so much a game of chance that it is difficult to attribute blame when all is not as it should be. If a virus has hit the stable and your horse has been one of the worst affected, there is no point in chastising the trainer, as long as he has taken all possible precautions. Neither are horses machines; they cannot be expected to perform well everytime, they too have off days and bloody-minded days. The more you are involved with horses, the more you will appreciate the problems of keeping a horse fit and well and ready to run.

Some horses (often called 'morning glories') work well at home, but are mere shadows of their former selves on the race-course. Others will be on line for a 'guaranteed' success, but will pull a muscle, puncture a foot or otherwise damage themselves, effectively putting themselves out of action for a while. The most frustrating horses are those that have a sixth sense for knowing when the big day is, and coughing a couple of times in front of the trainer a few days before the event. Some trainers take blood tests of the horses that are due to run the next day to make sure that the horses are well and not sickening for something.

Another possible source of discontent may be the staff who deal with your horse. For example, some trainers are very loyal to their stable jockeys, and rightly so in most cases; diplomacy is not the only desirable quality in a trainer, but if you are not happy with the way the jockey handles your horse, if, for instance he tends to over-use the whip, then you are perfectly entitled to engage another jockey. Unfortunately, such decisions can lead to friction in the yard over divided loyalties. A few trainers will stand by their jockey at the risk of losing an owner.

Personality clashes with the trainer himself or his wife are best solved by a change of yard. Moving the horse elsewhere may also be the answer if you feel you have given your trainer a fair chance to impress you, not necessarily with wins, but with his obvious attention to detail and perseverance, and he has failed.

Moving a horse from a yard poses practical as well as emotional problems. Your new trainer may let you have a horse-box to collect your horse from his old home. The horse may improve with a change of scenery, or may go into a decline because he misses his lad and his old routine. Therefore, whatever the effect of the move on the horse, give him time to settle in.

It is courteous to give your old trainer fair warning that you have decided to take the horse elsewhere so that he can start to find a replacement. A small trainer in particular will miss the income if a horse leaves, so be sure to tell him well in advance. Midnight raids will not be appreciated.

Removing your horse is the last resort and should of course be preceded by discussion, letting your trainer know your grievances and giving him a chance to act on them.

It will save a lot of argument if you both keep professional records of payment of training fees etc. Your Weatherbys account can see to this. It may also be helpful to befriend some of his other owners and compare costs to make sure that you are not picking up the feed bill for the entire yard, as happened to one foolish owner of the author's acquaintance!

The trainers are represented and assisted by the National Trainers' Federation, and if your trainer has a complaint against you as an owner, then he may approach the N.T.F. for advice before acting. You as an owner will be represented by the Racehorse Owners' Association based at 42 Portman Square, London W1, who will advise you on all matters of ownership. It is important that owners join the R.O.A. in order to give the Association a strong voice to defend the rights of owners on all matters that affect them. They will be fighting for you, so you would be wise to support them by becoming a member on payment of an annual fee. You will then have the peace of mind of knowing that an experienced team is ready and willing to assist you in your hour of need.

If you have a major problem, remember that grievances can usually be settled out of court, and, should it come to that, you may be glad that you did not take the trainer on as a partner in the ownership of the horse.

Learn from a nasty experience, and, if it does not put you off the sport, use that experience to help you find a more suitable trainer, with whose character you will not clash and whose aims are in unison with yours.

The Jockey Club, founded over 200 years ago, is racing's ruling body, which makes its own rules; the Rules of Racing. The Jockey Club's decision is usually final on racing matters. Entering races under the Rules of Racing creates a legal obligation to the Jockey Club, and owners agree to be bound by these Rules when they enter a horse. Any breaches of the Training Agreement will be dealt with by the Jockey Club, and the Club may 'warn off' owners, fine and suspend jockeys and suspend or withdraw training licences.

Try to ensure that, as an owner, things do not go wrong from your side; adhere to the rules of the sport and pay your bills. Owning a racehorse should then be an immensely enjoyable experience.

11 When the Horse is Finished on the Racecourse

Your horse's subsequent career may be restricted by the physical condition and the circumstances in which he ended his career as a racehorse. If the animal 'broke down' badly and the veterinary prognosis is not too hopeful, then all the horse will be good for in the near future is rest, but if he has done his best for you, and given you a lot of fun, then he deserves a rest. If his legs have taken a hammering whilst in training, which is highly likely if he started work as a two-year-old, he may never be sound enough for anything more demanding than gentle hacking around the lanes. However, this is a relaxing pastime and keeps you involved with your horse in his retirement. He certainly should not be turned out in a field and forgotten.

Another problem with horses that raced on the Flat as youngsters is that their skeletal frames have taken the work of a mature horse on immature bones, sometimes leading to problems later on in the horse's life. The young Thoroughbred lives a very unnatural life, geared towards maximum early growth, to the detriment of normal development. Horses would not normally be broken and backed until they were three or four years old, and then they would not be ridden strenuously, and certainly not galloped as a young racehorse is. Back problems seem quite common in the ex-racehorse as a direct result of being asked to do too much too soon, and recent research figures have shown that up to 50 per cent of horses off the racecourse have leg problems. However, there are other racehorses that will go through life unscathed by anything we ask of them, and still others will continue to approach any equestrian pastime at break-neck speed, never admitting that they are no longer on the racecourse. This can mean an exciting time is in store for those who take on retired racehorses.

If your horse ran in National Hunt races, it is less likely to have the aforementioned problems. The National Hunt horse's life is more in keeping with the natural development of the animal, allowing it to grow and gain the necessary strength needed to perform the tasks required of it. In some cases, however, the National Hunt fields are dotted with retired Flat horses, especially in hurdle races, so these horses may have started training as two-year-olds, and will continue to race over jumps well into equine middle age. To survive this early training and go on to more racing is the sign of a very resilient horse; the classic example being the record-breaking Grand National winner Red Rum who raced as a two-year-old and went from strength to strength, culminating in three victories and several placings in a steeplechaser's greatest test. Still active at the advanced age of 23 Red Rum is the exception to the rule.

National Hunt racing is a higher risk sport than the Flat, owing to the obstacles and other less skilled jumpers that the horse will encounter. It is this factor that possibly makes National Hunt racing a less reliable betting medium than the Flat. The best horse can fall or be brought down if a bad jumper interferes with him, and falls sustained at about 30 m.p.h. over stiff fences will tend to inflict injury to both man and beast. However, the tougher type of horse that tends to go over fences is less prone to everyday injury than the more lightly made, younger Flat racehorse.

National Hunt horses are also usually more sensible characters than their Flat-race counterparts, and will retire gracefully into the hunting field, giving their owner the thrill of the speed and jump exhibited on the racecourse in the past. The natural progression from this, if the old horse is up to it, is an assault on the point-to-point circuit.

Thoroughbreds are desirable competition horses in all fields of equestrianism because of their courage, speed, athleticism and quick reactions which can get them out of trouble and indeed into it, although their lack of calmness can sometimes be their downfall. It is their often intolerant 'fiery' temperaments that detract from their dressage performances, and they may have difficulty with the collected movements owing to their generally 'lengthy' conformation. The ex-point-to-pointer Wily Trout was an exception, however, and calmed down sufficiently

. . . its dressage test phase leaves something to be desired

to produce Olympic level dressage displays with his rider Christopher Bartle.

Event riders favour the Thoroughbred because of its speed and boldness across country, although, again, its dressage test phase often leaves something to be desired.

Top level showjumping also attracts the Thoroughbred where he comes into his own in classes against the clock. David Broome's Philco, retired from the American racetrack, was one of the most impressive examples of a racehorse adapting successfully to a new career.

Their good looks make Thoroughbreds attractive prospects for the show ring, especially in show hack and lightweight hunter classes. Again it is their temperaments that need working on rather than their gaits, which generally possess natural impulsion, and often too much of it!

To Breed or not to Breed

If you own a gelding, then your chances of breeding from him are effectively removed and you can start looking at one of the aforementioned pursuits for him. But a well-bred filly can be worth holding on to as a useful broodmare for the future. The plan with fillies destined for breeding is usually to try to win a small race and then pack them off to stud before their subsequent performances ruin the significance of their victory. However, the sporting owner who can afford to take the risk will keep his fillies in training for the good of the sport, to test their abilities properly.

Well-bred fillies can maintain their value as broodmares even if they show no great ability when in training, whereas a well-bred colt that fails as a racehorse may lose favour if he stands as a stallion, unless people are willing to send their mares to him in the hope that his breeding will overrule his own lack of talent.

In Tesio's book *Breeding the Racehorse* (J. A. Allen & Co.) he records some of the results of his research into breeding patterns and discovered that, on average, Thoroughbred broodmares give birth to more colts than fillies, ensuring that there is a certain amount of demand for the fillies for breeding purposes. The colts have to prove that they are worthy of being bred from, following a form of natural selection perhaps, where the larger numbers of colts leads to a chance to choose only the best as sires. The author has found no similar data to show whether this is still the trend in modern Thoroughbred breeding.

Sending your filly to the sales at the end of her three-year-old campaign could earn your money back, or maybe even a profit if you are lucky, if you do not wish to breed from her yourself. If you do wish to breed from her, consult a tax expert to advise you on this aspect of the industry as different rules apply to those of simply owning a horse in training.

It is to your advantage to convince the Inland Revenue that your breeding business is a business, and not a hobby, and the majority of private breeders do operate in the name of a company. If your stud does receive a hobby classification, then your expenses will not be tax deductible. A book to help you with the taxation aspect of ownership and breeding is *The H.A.C. Guide to Taxation of the Bloodstock Industry* by David Harris.

The cost of putting your filly to stud up to the time her three-year-old offspring is in training has been estimated at approximately £9,000. This will not include two more foals, a two-year-old in training or the cost of the stallion fees of the studs she will visit during that five year period.

Rearing a yearling for the sales would cost around £10,500, including the purchase of the in-foal mare, the keep of the mare and foal and the entry fee and preparation for the sales.

If you do embark on a breeding scheme, then you should consider the fact that you are setting yourself an impossible task; to control the uncontrollable. Breeders favour particular approaches, seeking to reproduce repeatable patterns in the pedigrees of bygone champions. Some even employ computers to add logic to their illogical assumptions. If their plans lead to one successful individual, then they reassert the importance of their theory, conveniently forgetting all the failures it took to produce one good horse. Horse breeding is subject to the laws of probability, as with the propagation of all species, and perseverance with almost any theory will eventually produce a success story, just as throwing three dice will eventually lead to three sixes coming up at the same time. It does not prove that the way you throw the dice is the best way. However, the book *Bloodstock Breeding* by Sir Charles Leicester (J. A. Allen & Co.) sets out the existing theories which make fascinating, if sometimes outrageous, reading.

In Darwin's work *The Origin of Species*, he proposed that 'Natural Selection' takes place whereby those animals best suited to their life styles and environment are selected for breeding and those less well suited to the lives they lead are not selected, thus ensuring that the best qualities spread within the species' population. The horse breeder imposes artificial selection on his horses, selecting for characteristics that he values such as speed, stamina and soundness.

Mendel's laws of inheritance can apply as much to horse breeding as they do to the peas which he studied in his original work. He states that genes from the sire and dam can combine in several ways to produce certain characteristics in the offspring. To add to the interest, some genes are dominant and some are recessive, thus, as their names imply, dominant genes are able to override the influence of recessive genes, leading to the dominant characteristic occurring in the offspring. For example, the gene for normal ears in the horse is dominant over the genes for droopy ears, so if the dam has normal ears, and the sire has droopy ears, then the offspring will have a 3 : 1 chance of having normal ears. Such laws apply to coat colour and most other characteristics (although I have simplified the situation for ease of understanding), but these do not appear to apply to the inheritance of speed in the same logical sequence. However, the laws do apply to the factors that can combine to lead to speed; factors such as type of muscle fibre, shape of leg etc.

If you are breeding for the racing market, then you will feel pressurised to send your mare to one of the 'in vogue' stallions, as the offspring of such couplings will command a decent price. Unfortunately, the more popular a stallion becomes, the more successful he will appear to be and the stud fee will shoot up. If you can afford to send your mare to such an expensive Romeo, and his connections regard your mare as a worthy Juliet, then fine. The cost can be reduced slightly if you go to a stud where no mares are resident, a stud where the mare is taken to the stallion when she is in season, covered and taken home again. This is called the 'walk-in' system and is becoming popular in America. This obviously removes the fee for accommodation, although it may mean that you have to drive your mare to the stallion again if she is found not to be in foal the first time. If you cannot afford one of the fancy stallions, then you must do some astute research.

The solution would be to select a stallion that is unfashionable at the moment, but looks as if he will make his mark in the near future. Genetically speaking, every stallion has the 'potential' to be as good as Northern Dancer, so all stallions standing will need close inspection. You might reduce the list by narrowing the field to those horses standing within a certain mile radius from your home base. Choose those which are strong in conformation where your mare is weak. If the mare has cow hocks and the stallion has particularly good hind legs, then he must be a possibility. Look at third generation sires, visit some and follow the two-year-olds that emerge from those sires. Look at the average and median prices for the offspring to gauge the value of the animal as a cross. Someone had to be the first to send their mare to Northern Dancer, not knowing how well he would do as

If the mare has cow hocks . . .

a sire, so it is always a gamble. Remember *all* stallions produce more average horses than good ones.

The problem with breeding racehorses, is that you will spend a lot of money on the stud fee, veterinary treatment and rearing the foal; money which you will need to regain in the selling price of the youngster as well as making a profit. Struggling breeders may not even recoup the stud fee on the sale of their produce. The trend has been for fewer people to take up ownership, so the market for your product is getting smaller. There are, however, signs of an upward trend appearing again. Breeding horses can actually cost you a considerable amount of money, and is not the kind of business in which to make millions from nothing unless you are extraordinarily lucky. To keep up to date on breeding matters, it may be worth your while to join the Thoroughbred Breeders' Association, based in Newmarket.

If you are comfortable enough financially not to have to worry about such details, then there must be few other things as rewarding in life as breeding your mare to your choice of stallion, and hoping and waiting for the offspring to be a world beater, or just a healthy happy horse. Few mares will produce winners as consistently as Lord and Lady Tavistock's Mrs. Moss, but you never know till you try.

The situation that must be avoided is the flooding of the market with unwanted young horses whose fates are not assured.

Having catered for your retired filly, what do you do with the retired colt? If he has been a flop as a racehorse and has unpopular breeding, then you might decide to take the twinkle out of his eye. As a gelding, he might settle down and prove to be a better racehorse, once he has wiped the look of indignation off his face. If he was average on the Flat, then he might improve over hurdles, giving him a new lease of life, or if he dislikes hurdling it may put him off racing forever.

In the rare event that your colt is an attractive stallion prospect, having enjoyed Group One success or similar, and being fashionably bred, then you may wish to syndicate your stallion, selling shares in him. These shares will capitalise into forty nomination fees i.e., the buyers of these shares will be buying the right to have one of their mares visit the stallion each season. If the owner of a share does not have a mare to send one season, then he can sell that year's nomination to someone else. This is obviously the most lucrative way to earn money from a racehorse. For example, Dancing Brave had his shares on offer for a reported £350,000 each. The animal's prize money may be only a fraction of his syndication fee. The shareholders are usually vetted first to ensure that they can pay the fee and that they have suitable mares who complement the stallion's qualities to produce a good cross.

A stallion that is not as nicely related as the bloodstock industry would like, but is a well made, sound individual of good size and substance, may prosper under the Hunter Improvement Society scheme which approves good stallions for breeding competition horses. Such stallions will probably not serve many Thoroughbred mares, but will add class and quality to a lesser-bred mare's offspring.

Stallions may prove themselves great sires of jumpers; Deep Run has an impressive record in the production of National Hunt horses, including Gold Cup and Champion Hurdle heroine Dawn Run. The Flat racehorse that sires National Hunt horses may be regarded as something of a failure by his connections, but may become a legend through his jumping offspring. Unfortunately, a sire of jumpers may be very old or dead before

90

his prowess is recognised, because it takes so much longer to see if jumpers are successful. Jumpers do not tend to sire jumpers because the vast majority of male horses running under National Hunt rules are gelded to lessen the risk of injury to their undercarriages and to produce a quieter, easier to handle race-horse.

The idea in Thoroughbred breeding is to breed the best with the best, but with the trend being to remove horses to stud after their three-year-old racing season it means that we never actually know if these youngsters really are the best horses. It would be easier to tell if the breed was improving if horses were tested for racing ability fully before being retired to stud. Certainly it would appear that something is wrong with our current breeding and training methods. Human running times have increased in speed without specific mating strategies, the four minute mile being a regular occurrence now amongst athletes. Trotters' times have also improved, but, although there was an initial increase in speed at the inception of the Thoroughbred breed, the Flat racehorse's speeds have not increased over the last 50 years.

The speed plateau may reflect the possibility that the Thoroughbred has reached its pinnacle as a breed for speed. Perhaps the Thoroughbred cannot improve any more, with its frame unable to bear a faster and more stressful gallop. This is probably due to a combination of our breeding regimes and our training practices, or may just be nature's way of controlling unnatural and perhaps unhealthy advances.

Scientists working on equine fitness have shown that horses are unable to control their breathing at faster gaits, because the action of the gallop forces the diaphragm up into the lungs, leading to shallow breathing. Thus, unlike man, the horse cannot breath well at a fast run. The horse overcomes this lack of oxygen by releasing haemoglobin (oxygen carrying) blood cells from the spleen into the bloodstream to supply the muscles until the horse slows down again and can once again breath normally. Thus, to train sprinters successfully this would suggest that one should concentrate on facilitating this release from the spleen which will not occur in slow, stamina-building exercise. Modern training methods send sprinters out on slow exercise mixed with fast work, which, according to the physiological findings, will actually inhibit the efficient release of oxygen-carrying cells into the blood. If sprinters are only allowed to sprint, then their times should theoretically improve because they are being trained specifically for the job, however, the horse's legs would take a hammering from such practices. It has yet to be described by physiologists as to how a sprinter can maintain a purely sprinting workload without suffering physical stress and strain on the limbs and joints. Perhaps we should be breeding for a particular type of spleen! The sports medicine practitioners think they have found the solution in their interval training systems. Whatever the answer, the Thoroughbred breed is not progressing at the rate that it has done in the past.

When your horse has retired from public life, and as long as he is fit and well he can go on for many years. The only problem facing you will be whether or not to start all over again with a new horse, new trainer perhaps and maybe new partners, but with the same old dreams. You will find owning a racehorse quite addictive, perhaps financially challenging and you will, hopefully, gain a lot of pleasure and satisfaction from it. You will also be that much closer to understanding why they call horse racing the Sport of Kings.

12 Books the Racehorse Owner Will Find Helpful

Some of the books mentioned in this chapter are annuals and became out of date at the end of the year or season, therefore when the year is mentioned in the title of a book, the date has been omitted to avoid confusion.

Your bible must be the *Rules of Racing*, produced by the Jockey Club via Weatherbys' publication department. The Rules are updated and revised each year and become available at around the start of the Flat season. This is a small but essential book, the book that the owner and most definitely the trainer must have on his writing desk. A glance at the Rules is all that is required to avoid treading on Stewards' toes with regard to what should and should not be done in racing in this country.

Another requisite is the *Racing Calendar* for deciding on which races to enter. The trainer may be quite generous with your money when it comes to entering your horse, so it may be worth your while to keep track of these expenses and be ready to curtail any unnecessary entry enthusiasm. If, for example, the horse will obviously not run if the stable jockey that you favour cannot ride him, or because you as the owner have no intention of travelling to some of the more distant tracks, then stop the entry. You also have the right to refuse to run your horse at a course you dislike on whatever grounds, without feeling guilty, after all, you are paying to enjoy owning a racehorse and if you cannot see it race, then why bother?

The *Racing Calendar* is the official publication for Jockey Club notices as well as containing details of races, conditions, entries, forfeits, acceptances, weights, results, meetings, names of horses in training etc. It will provide information on 'warned off' individuals and other results of transgressions of the Rules of Racing. It also contains the up-to-date handicap ratings.

In the late eighteenth century a man called Weatherby

93

decided to record the births and matings of all Thoroughbred horses, producing a volume called the *General Stud Book*. The Weatherby family company still produces this publication today and have thus provided an invaluable service to the Thoroughbred industry. The *General Stud Book* lists all Thoroughbred broodmares in alphabetical order, giving their progeny, including date of birth, sex and colour of foal, name (when the horse is old enough), name of the breeder (i.e. owner of the mare when each foal was born) and the name of the sire. The *General Stud Book* is now in two handsome volumes that are bound in leather in either full- or half-calf editions. The *General Stud Book* is produced every four years.

If a mare was barren, lost her foal or produced twins, this will also be recorded. Therefore, to look a horse up in the *General Stud Book*, you need to know the dam's name for all unnamed horses, although named horses are indexed. The supplement to the *General Stud Book* is the annual publication, again by Weatherbys, called *The Statistical Record Annual Return of Mares*. This will also supply the stallion fertility ratings. This publication becomes available in November each year.

The Statistical Record Annual provides the statistics of Flat race breeding to the end of December each year. The winning distances of sires' progeny are given, which would help you to choose a suitable horse to put your filly to. The number of winners and placed horses in Great Britain and abroad are also given under each sire enabling lists of 'top sires' to be compiled.

The National Hunt equivalent of this is *The Statistical Record Jump Annual*, which gives similar statistics for jump racing from the start of January to the end of December, and includes the leading sires of point-to-pointers and hunterchasers.

To follow your horse's form, or to research the prowess of a potential purchase, study the *Raceform Flat Annual* or *Chaseform Annual* for the equivalent National Hunt information. These will supply the details of the horse's performances for the previous season. The horse will be listed for each race he took part in, the position in which he finished, the weight he carried, the starting price, who the jockey was, the meeting, the name of the race, the going, the distance, the weather conditions and a brief abbreviated description of the sort of race he ran. There are a couple of other annual publications that serve the same purpose:

The Sporting Life Flat Results in Full and the National Hunt equivalent. These two publications also include the Irish results.

Another way to learn about the horse's race record is to obtain a copy of Phil Bull's Timeform Annual *Racehorses of . . .* for the Flat, or *Chasers and Hurdlers* for the National Hunt. The Flat annuals originally emerged as *Best Horses* annuals in the 1940s. The *Chasers and Hurdlers* began later on in the 1970s. It is becoming very popular amongst racing people to collect these annuals and full sets may be valuable.

These glossy volumes will have a rating for the horses that have raced that year, listing them in alphabetical order, with essays, photographs and pedigrees on the most successful horses that season. The ratings reflect how much weight each horse would have to carry if they were all to race against each other in one huge cavalry charge and come across the line together in a free handicap race! Obviously those with the highest rating are the best horses, which would be given the most weight to carry. The very best horses are rated in the 140s including such notables as Shergar rated 140, Ribot rated 142 and Brigadier Gerard rated 144. The ratings are higher for the National Hunt horses.

Owners will probably regard their horses as having been unkindly rated, being particularly offended if an 'ungenuine' squiggle accompanies the rating figure. But Timeform Annuals are renowned for their accuracy and good objective judgement (with the odd exception of course). They do not generally rate below 40.

Timeform also produces the weekly *Black Book* which gives ratings for the horses that have raced so far this season. They also produce the daily racecards that can be bought at the racecourse as well as from specialist retailers.

An annual publication called *Horses in Training* lists practically all the horses in training under the names of their trainers. The owner's name appears by the side of his horse, along with the animal's sire and dam. Unnamed two-year-olds will be listed under their breeding and sex. A glance at the list of names of the owners with a trainer may help you to decide when looking for a suitable trainer, crossing out the trainers with the owners you wish to avoid by a process of elimination! *Horses in*

Training also gives the names of the jockeys and apprentices employed by the trainer.

The Trainers' Record is produced for both the Flat and National Hunt trainers, and analyses their training strengths and weaknesses of the past season. Again, a study of such a book may help you to pick your type of trainer, or at least help you to eliminate a few.

Just before the beginning of the Flat season, the *Programme of Meetings for the Flat* is issued, giving the dates and entry details and values of the races for the forthcoming season. If you wish to be able to discuss the placing of your horse in races with your trainer, then this book will enable you to do so knowledgeably. It can help you to isolate the meetings that you will or will not be able to attend and to enter the horse accordingly. The equivalent *National Hunt Programme* is produced in two volumes, coming out a few months apart.

A most useful book for the owner is the *Directory of the Turf*, produced annually, which lists names, addresses and telephone numbers of everyone you could wish to contact in the bloodstock and racing world, from specialists in equine insurance to apprentice jockeys. It gives small biographies of the trainers, jockeys and owners of note, listing their racing interests, their best horses, trained, ridden or owned, and perhaps even a favourite hobby.

When owners' thoughts turn to the idea of breeding with their horse, a useful publication to examine would be the *Bloodstock Sales Review and Stud Register* which provides the auction records, the vendors, the purchasers and the price in guineas of horses sold. The average yearling and foal prices are given in alphabetical order of stallion, giving the number of lots sold, the total price achieved in guineas, the highest and average price paid.

Sires of . . . is an international guide to the stallions standing at stud. Some of the top English and Irish stallions are listed in the *Stallion Book for . . .* which gives a full page photograph of the stallion and a detailed report of his racing activities and breeding success to date.

The monthly magazine *Pacemaker* is useful for racing issues and news, and the quarterly *European Racehorse* magazine (originally called the *British Racehorse*) is aimed at those whose main interest is breeding.

A book to provide you with a sound grounding in the theories of bloodstock breeding is the classic work by Sir Charles Leicester, *Bloodstock Breeding*, which has been revised and updated by Howard Wright.

The daily racing papers include *The Sporting Life* and its younger rival *The Racing Post*, both of which will provide details of the previous day's race results, the day's card and the entries and declarations for the following day's racing, 'naps', or tips, for horses, interviews with racing personalities, breeding analyses and racing gossip.

13 Questions on Racing

In this chapter I have endeavoured to anticipate some of the questions that the prospective owner might wish to ask. The answers are from individuals experienced in their respective fields, but their opinions are personal and may not be concurred with by everyone within those fields.

I hope the reader will have slightly fewer questions to ask after reading the following pages.

The Trainer

Answers from Charles Nelson of Kingsdown stables, Lambourn.

Q.   Do you buy horses before finding owners for them?

A.   Only if I feel a horse I like is very good value will I buy it and then pass it on to an owner.

Q.   How do you go about acquiring owners?

A.   Owners go to trainers, and the best way of acquiring owners is by having winners. A new owner is sometimes attracted by buying in to a horse.

Q.   What is the most convenient type of ownership from the trainer's point of view, the individual or larger group?

A.   Individual, but partnerships can be more fun if the partners are already friends.

Q.   Do you encourage your owners to visit the yard and see their horse(s) on a regular basis, perhaps setting aside specific times?

A.   My owners can come at any time and we are pleased to see them.

Q.   How much of your time is taken up by entertaining and advising your owners in an average working day?

A.   Apart from the training quite a bit of time is taken up by advising owners, and selling off bloodstock when their best results have been achieved on the racecourse.

Q.   Do you like to discuss the entries you are making with the owner when possible?

A.   My owners leave it to me, but I do discuss entries when the entry fees are high, for Group races etc.

Q.   At the races do you feel responsible for the owner's enjoyment and feel obliged to entertain them?

A.   I feel it is important to give owners the most pleasure possible from owning a horse, and quite often new and foreign owners are not sure what to do or where to go to find the best place from which to see a race.

Q.   What do you see as your duties to owners?

A.   Giving them as much pleasure as possible and doing the best for the horse.

Q.   How do you settle on the fee you charge?

A.   You do get what you pay for in life, and, although owners require value for money, a yard with enough staff and the right facilities makes it more expensive.

Q.   Would you welcome the advertising of trainer's fees, or is it a case of if you have to ask you cannot afford it?

A.   I have never thought about advertising fees, although most owners do ask the cost.

Q.   Do trainers prefer horsemen as owners who will appreciate the problems of training horses, or do they like owners who may be less technically aware of what is involved?

A.   Sometimes it is a little easier to have a horseman, but sometimes a little knowledge is a dangerous thing.

Q.   Do you provide livery for your horses out of season, or do your owners make their own arrangements?

A.   We do not provide livery. While the horses are here they are classed as being in training.

Q.   Do your owners give you a free hand in sending their horses abroad to race?

A.   Yes, as long as the cost is reasonable and I believe the horse has a good chance of winning.

Q.   Would you prefer a potential owner to contact you before he has acquired a horse?

A.   I like to be involved in choosing the horse myself right from the start.

Q.   Do you refer your owners to bloodstock agents when they approach you wanting to purchase a horse?

A.   I work with a bloodstock agent at the sales, but my owners are not referred to one; they buy through me.

Q.   Do you see part of your role towards owners as a P.R. job?

A.   Sometimes, mainly at meetings. Owners like being told on the spot information about the race, the other runners etc. and generally being looked after.

Q.   Do you feel it your duty to let an owner know when his horse is not coming up to scratch and suggest he sells it?

A.   Yes. If a horse is of very limited ability and has very little hope of winning any races, I suggest it is sold or retires to stud as it is in the owner's and trainer's interest to, hopefully, replace it with a new horse that could win races and justify the expense of keeping it in training.

Q.   How would you feel about an owner that wanted to ride his horse in amateur races?

A.   O.K. if he is a good enough rider, if not I would not run the horse and risk losing my licence to train.

Q.   In general, if there was a difference of opinion between one of your owners and a member of your staff, who would your loyalties be with?

A.   This obviously depends on the situation and this is where the P.R. comes in.

Q.   Do you feel that a successful trainer is entitled to share in the stud value of the horses he trains?

A.   It depends on the original arrangements made.

Q.   Would you actively put people together with the aim of forming partnerships to keep a horse or horses with you?

A.   Yes. The price of horses can go up considerably if successful and the risk of losing a large increase in tax free capital can be too great for a smaller owner. So quite often I put together a partnership with larger owners so he gains cash and still retains an interest.

Q. *Do you like to retain a share in the horses in training with you?*

A. If I like a yearling enough and feel that we bought very well, I would take a share if invited to do so.

Q. *Do owners ever ask you to run a horse in a race where it is obviously misplaced?*

A. No. Every horse should be given the best possible chance of winning and although we may run with an outside chance, nothing is ever gained by running with no chance.

[A prime example is Bellefella, a 100-1 shot for the 1988 2000 Guineas, who certainly did not disgrace himself by coming third for Mr. Nelson.]

Q. *Do some owners refuse to have their horses sent to distant race courses because it is inconvenient for them?*

A. Yes. A lot of owners would rather sell and buy again than travel hundreds of miles away which is expensive and involves them in long journeys which they may not have the time to do.

Q. *Do new owners tend to expect success too soon?*

A. All owners like to see their horses run as soon as possible, but tend to take a trainer's advice that their horse is too immature or weak and would not benefit from being run too early. The horse may, in fact, lose strength if run too soon.

Q. *Is there any type of horse that you would not take on if an owner presented you with it?*

A. Yes. A lunatic!

Q. *What advice would you give to someone contemplating racehorse ownership?*

A. Go and meet as many trainers as possible and put your horse with the one you enjoyed being with the most. Fun is a very important factor. Also choose someone you may have respected as a trainer of good horses. Owning a racehorse must be a hobby first and foremost. You should only go in at a comfortable level, where you may regard the training fees as taking up fun money and the horse as an investment in what is a high-risk business.

The Bloodstock Agent

Answers from Susan Cameron of Sagittarius Bloodstock, London.

Q. *How much emphasis do you put on the pedigree of a horse when choosing a horse for a client?*

A. Quite a bit. The customer who specifies the sex of horse that they want governs how much emphasis is put on the pedigree. For the first time owner, I would always recommend that they buy fillies with good pedigrees to ensure paddock value. Such fillies will sell on or can be used by the owner himself as brood-mares. One takes more risk in buying colts. Bad racing fillies with good pedigrees are still reasonably valuable, but bad colts are bad news.

Q. *What type of horse would you recommend for a newcomer to race-horse ownership?*

A. It depends on the owner. If he is impatient to get started, then you cannot buy him a Classic-potential horse, which will possibly not even run as a two-year-old, so it depends on the owner's need for an immediate runner.

  If the owner wants a horse for jumping, then it will probably be cheaper to buy a hurdler than a 'chaser who has been especially bred for the job. The suitable physical characteristics are essential in the National Hunt type, and often more important than the pedigree.

Q. When an owner comes to you with a price limit, how do you proceed to buy a horse for them?

A. We peruse the sales catalogues. Private sales are sometimes too expensive, so we would tend to go to a public auction. It is really all a matter of being at the right place at the right time when buying horses. Only if the customer is in a real hurry would we buy privately. Hunting down a suitable animal can take from days to months. A horse's potential is more expensive than performance. At the sales you have more choice and you know the price at the end of the bidding. Private sales may set a price way above the real value the same horse would make at auction.

Q. Will you accept work from owners who approach you direct, or do you prefer to be introduced by someone established in the racing world?

A. We are happy to be approached direct. We are a member of the Federation of Bloodstock Agents, so there is a standard that we work to, and clients know what to expect from us.

Q. Is there a price level below which you will not work?

A. We have no lower limit and will accept commissions from buyers with relatively small amounts to spend. Some bloodstock agents charge a minimum of £100, but as yet we have no set lower limit. We try to take time and trouble with all our clients, hopefully building up good will and perhaps leading to another buy in the future. We have had people consult us for years without buying anything, and then suddenly they turn up with some money to spend on a racehorse. You cannot really class any customer as a time-waster.

. . . suddenly they turn up with some money . . .

Q. *Would you advise the first time racehorse owner to go to a blood-stock agent or rely on his trainer for choosing a horse?*

A. Either, as long as you take care in choosing whichever one. You are possibly better off with a professional agent than some trainers, although this sounds biased! It is best to get personal recommendation from others with experience of that particular agent or trainer. Trainers often work in conjunction with an agent who is more aware of market values.

Q. *What do you look for when assessing a horse for the Flat?*

A. I always look at the horses regardless of their pedigree; we have chosen horses on conformation alone. The general impression the horse gives is very important. We assess the overall look and then dissect it. We like to see a generous eye and good limbs. Some defects can be excused, especially if you are buying for yourself, but defects can be difficult when buying for a client. We try to buy 'correct types' who have overall good conformation. Legs are particularly important as the car is no good without wheels! However, defects tend to disappear in the winner's enclosure! The agent stakes his professional reputation every time he makes a purchase, so he has to take trouble over it and know what he is doing.

Q. What do you look for when assessing a horse for National Hunt?

A. A bigger boned animal than for the Flat. It must be bold and have the right attitude in the ring. If the horse is to be a hurdler, then we look at its Flat race record. One looks more at the pedigree for steeplechasers than hurdlers. Horses well-bred for 'chasing will attract money where there may be no race experience to go on.

Q. Is the newcomer best advised to go to one of the big established bloodstock agencies, or to go to one of the smaller, perhaps more personal agencies?

A. It depends on the funds available. Bigger agencies may be less enthusiastic over smaller sums. If the buyer does not have much money to spend, I would suggest that he goes to one of the smaller agents who have smaller costs and overheads to cover.

Q. Are there suitable horses at more sensible prices now after the bloodstock boom of recent years?

A. Prices are more realistic now. It has always been possible to buy decent horses anyway and one can only hope that the stallion fees will come down to help the breeders as well. Good horses can be bought in almost every price range. A few years ago we bought a client a horse for the Derby for 5,000 guineas which was our client's limit. The horse did run in the Derby and beat eight of his expensive rivals. In real terms, no horse is worth some of the high price tags of recent years.

Q. If a particular customer wanted a particular horse and had given you a limit, would you exceed the limit to secure the horse?

A. We did once and it worked out well, but you would have to know your client well before doing so. You cannot take liberties.

One would not exceed the limit with a new client. We can usually assess prices quite accurately, but there are always some surprises. You can start assessing the price that youngstock will fetch by working from the stallion nomination fee.

Q. Do you regard entering into racehorse ownership as a sound business move?

A. No definitely not. The old saying is true that you can come out of racing with a small fortune, but only having gone in with a large one. One should really go in for fun. Racehorse ownership can be a good company move for advertising and entertaining guests. It is better for a company to own several horses in the hope that one might be good enough for them to break even over all.

Q. Who are bloodstock agents and how are they qualified to do their job?

A. There is no standard training course. Most are horsemen with a bit of business sense. Most start working with other agents and then branch out on their own. It is a bit like a travelling circus, with everyone meeting up at the sales all around the world.

Q. In general, what do you look for in the conformation of a horse?

A. A good front with a nice shoulder and good length of rein (neck), good limbs, but above all, the way the horse uses himself. One rarely sees a nicely balanced horse on the racecourse, and many trainers do not seem to know how to balance a horse, getting the hocks to come underneath the body and enhance the propulsion effect of the hind legs. A lot of young horses are so unbalanced that they cannot take corners, so become one-sided, unable to cope with left- or right-handed courses. A horse that is in control of his body, and with the centre of gravity in the right place, is at a distinct advantage.

Q. Would you recommend that an owner acquires a foal or a yearling to send Flat racing later on?

A. In most cases I would recommend purchasing a yearling as it saves a year's keep costs and reduces the risk of injury. It is not usually worth the risk of buying a foal as it is very difficult to judge how it will develop in two years' time. We carried out a survey that showed that people will pay more for a foal than a yearling by the same sire, which seems totally illogical. Some people specialise in buying foals and selling them on as yearlings, hoping to make a rapid profit on their initial outlay. In America such people used to produce their yearlings in gross condition, although this craze seems to be dying out thankfully.

Q. Why do you think so many owners drop out every year? Is it purely financial?

A. Mainly financial as it is not easy to continue in the present financial climate. Some get disillusioned, probably due to lack of care at the start when they were choosing their associates. Racing needs to look after the smaller owner, treating them well and hoping they will stay and continue to support the sport.

Q. What advice would you give to owners wishing to breed from their colt/filly?

A. Do not breed from a horse without good pedigree or performance. It may be worth a try if the horse is either well-bred or ran well, preferably both. Expert advice is needed to decide who to send your mare to. You should decide first whether you will race the offspring or sell them. If you are keeping them yourself, then you can breed anything you like. If you are breeding to sell, then you must follow the trends. You must work three years ahead to when your offspring will be selling.

Q. Would you recommend that a newcomer to ownership, planning a large bloodstock enterprise takes on a bloodstock agent to act as a racing manager?

A. If inexperienced themselves, then I would recommend that they use an agent who will do all the planning and paperwork and will liaise with the trainer(s). There is no standard rate for managing as there is with buying, so you may need to shop around. It depends on the level of involvement. Proven managers will charge more, but are usually worth it, whereas someone who may know racing but has never managed before, could be more of a risk.

Q. *What information do you particularly note in the sales catalogue?*

A. It depends on what you are buying. If you can spend a large amount then one will look for a lot of black type. If buying a yearling, look for a family that can run and win modest races. Sound and fertile families are desirable. We are most interested in the first and second dam in the pedigree. It is always nice to see mares producing good stock from moderate stallions.

Q. *What other advice would you give to someone considering entering into ownership?*

A. Set yourself realistic expectations; the main aim always being to have fun. The Sangster machine is a different ball game. If you intend to emulate such business approaches, then the money must be there first. With the right publicity colts can be valued way above their true worth making them seem much better stud prospects than they actually are.

As long as you go in for fun, then you should not be disappointed.

The Owner

Answers from Terry Jennings, a quite newly established owner, owning the winner of the Wokingham Handicap at Royal Ascot, Touch of Grey, and the owner of Watermill stud, Thetford, Norfolk.

Q. *How did you become interested in owning racehorses?*

A. Through a friend. I had been interested in going to the races and knew a number of people who had an interest in racing, but it was only when I was actually offered a horse myself that I decided to give it a try.

Q. How did you choose your trainer?

A. By personal contact, and straight talking. It is important to ensure that you select a trainer you can get on with and trust! Make your wishes clear from the start so that you understand each other's viewpoint. Look at the trainer's track record, number and type of horse and decide if this is your man. If you do not trust him, it will not work.

Q. How did you acquire your first horse?

A. I was offered a horse by an acquaintance. I had little knowledge of breeding or of horse values, so I contacted a friend who owned a number of horses for advice. Clearly this advice was essential since the horse I was offered was over-priced and I declined the offer. My friend then suggested that if I wanted to buy a horse I would do better to speak to a trainer. I subsequently purchased a yearling which the trainer had in his yard.

Q. Being personally involved in outright ownership, partnership and company ownership, could you outline the advantages and disadvantages of each.

A. Personal ownership has the advantage of it being 'your horse'. The horse runs in your colours and you have all the prize money or increase in the value of the horse, if either apply. The big disadvantage is that you also have all the costs and this must be taken into account. Probably the total cost of having a horse in training in the Newmarket area is now in the region of £9,000 a year when you take into account all extras, so, because of the costs, it does make good sense to consider other forms of ownership.

Having a share in a horse is a good alternative. This is

normally for two to four people. The obvious advantage of this is that the costs reduce proportionally. This type of ownership is ideal for friends or relations who get on very well and have the same attitude towards the horse. The difficulty can be when there is disagreement over whether a horse should run, be sold, be gelded etc. For this reason I believe that all decisions relating to the horse in the case of a partnership should be in the hands of one person - preferably the trainer. It is most important that such things are discussed and agreed at the beginning. It must also be decided in whose colours a horse should run, or, alternatively, colours can be registered in joint names.

The extended partnership is similar in a way to a partnership except that numbers are greater, and it is, therefore, even more important that the decisions be made by one person on behalf of the group. Also all members should liaise through one member. A trainer does not want 12 different people calling him about one horse.

Company ownership has recently increased dramatically. There are two kinds of company ownership. The first is when a company decides to own a horse for promotional purposes and the horse may be named after a product of the company, or the venture may be used to entertain customers at the races. The other kind of company ownership is when a company is formed specifically to enable members to become the registered owners of a racehorse. This allows a greater number of people than 12 to have an interest in a racehorse. The horse(s) are owned by the company and the company is owned by its members or shareholders. Hence a share in such a company gives a share also in the company's assets - the horses. Again the advantage of this type of ownership is that the costs of horseracing can be divided into any number of shareholders. There are a number of companies who operate quite successfully in this way and the directors do a good job in administering the day to day business and keeping the members informed. However, there are also other companies that are formed simply to make a profit for the directors and it is important to choose the right company before getting involved.

The money that a shareholder puts in to one of these companies should be deemed as an 'investment' for the fun derived from the involvement.

Q.   Do you regard your racing as a hobby or a business?

A.   A hobby! Only a fool would regard racing as a business if he is a small owner. The chance of a horse ever making a profit is extremely low. In an ideal world prize money would at least cover the costs, but even if you are fortunate enough to have a horse that wins a race, it is still unlikely that it will cover its costs.

Q.   What was your motivation for setting up a racehorse-owning company?

A.   The only way that most people can have an interest in a number of horses is through multiple ownership. It was a compromise for me to set up a racing company to enable me to have the cost shared of racing several horses. In that respect my initial motivation was probably quite selfish. However I quickly learned that it can be quite fun to get a number of people together with the same interest. A racing group-ownership can lead to more enjoyment at a more reasonable price. In my own case, I am content to see the company evolving into a small 'club'.

Q.   What is your opinion of the increasing number of racing companies that are springing up, offering smaller shares to larger numbers of people?

A.   Anything that promotes racehorse ownership must be good for the industry. My only reservation about the increasing number of racing companies is that they are not all being run for the sole benefit of the members. There are some good ones and some not so good. I believe there is likely to be more monitoring of racing companies' activities by the Jockey Club and there may be some changes in the near future. They are also technically difficult to administer due to company law being what it is. There are sure to be changes in the future. Good racing companies should be encouraged.

Q.   What procedure would you recommend for those considering buying shares in a racing company?

A. Obtain all available prospectuses and compare them with each other. Look at the names of the directors and their interests and ask why they are doing it. What payments are being made to directors or employees? How are the horses being bought and sold and what independent horse values are obtained? What is your interest in racing? Ownership can lead to information for gambling and for social get-togethers. In all cases always consider the money spent.

Q. Would you advocate sharing a horse with a trainer?

A. Yes. If a trainer is prepared to retain an interest in a horse then he must think it a worthwhile risk. However, there are a small number of trainers who would retain a minority share in almost any horse, just to sell the remaining interest to a potential owner (at an inflated price sometimes) to obtain training fees for another horse. A good test is to ask the trainer if he would retain 50 per cent.

Q. What effect do you think group ownership has on racing?

A. Group ownership certainly must mean that more people attend the races and take a greater interest generally. More horses are in training than there would be otherwise, which must be a help to the trainers and the industry generally. It is also likely that a small number of people will progress to become owners in their own right as their circumstances improve, or their liking for the sport grows.

I do not think that multiple ownership necessarily means a loss of prestige to racing, so much as the bad behaviour of a minority of people often does.

Q. What would your advice be to someone considering taking a share in a horse?

A. Count your available money first. Calculate the capital costs and the full training expenses for a year, and be prepared to write that off in full. You can pay £50,000 for a horse which a year later is worth £500. The whole exercise should be looked at as an experience.

Don't gamble more than a few pounds for the fun of it. Obviously you want to have a flutter on your horse, but do not get carried away. The expense of horse racing is prohibitive enough without adding to it by losing large sums of money to the bookies. If tipsters, owners or even trainers were able to be that sure, they would not need you to support them.

Buy your horse or share from the trainer you have selected. If he has not got one, ask him for advice. Be pleased if he asks for more than he paid for the horse, because he has to make a profit and it is better that you can see where he is doing it.

14 Useful Addresses

British Bloodstock Agency plc
Queensberry House, High Street, Newmarket, Suffolk CB8 9BD.

British Bloodstock Agency (Ireland) Ltd.
51 Lansdowne Road, Ballsbridge, Dublin 4, Ireland.

Curragh Bloodstock Agency Ltd.
Newbridge, Co. Kildare, Ireland.

Federation of Bloodstock Agents (G.B.) Ltd.
The Old Brewery, Hampton Street, Tetbury, Gloucestershire GL8 8TG.

Jockeys' Association of G.B. Ltd.
1 Bridge Street, Newbury, Berkshire RG14 5BE.

Jockey Club
42 Portman Square, London W1H 0EN.

National Trainers' Federation
42 Portman Square, London W1H 0AP.

Charles Nelson (trainer)
Kingsdown, Upper Lambourn, Newbury, Berkshire.

Pratt & Co.
11 Boltro Road, Haywards Heath, Sussex RH16 1BP.

Raceform Ltd.
29 York Road, London SW11.

Racehorse Owners' Association
42 Portman Square, London W1H 9FF.

Racing Post
Cannon House, 112-120 Coombe Lane, Raynes Park, London SW20 0BA.

Sagittarius Bloodstock Agency
44 Conway Road, London N15 3BA.

Sporting Life
Alexander House, 81-9 Farringdon Road, London EC1M 3HJ.

Tattersalls Ltd.
Terrace House, Newmarket, Suffolk CB8 9BT.

Thoroughbred Breeders' Association
Stanstead House, The Avenue, Newmarket, Suffolk CB8 9AA.

Timeform
Timeform House, Northgate, Halifax, Yorkshire HX1 1XE.

Weatherbys
42 Portman Square, London W1H 0EN.

Weatherbys Publications
Sanders Road, Wellingborough, Northamptonshire NN8 4BX.